13 <u>95</u>

The Feast of Friendship

The Feast of Friendship

by

Paul D. O'Callaghan

The Feast of Friendship

Eighth Day Press

2838 E. Douglas Ave. Wichita, KS 67214

1-800-841-2541

ISBN 0-9717483-0-6

LCCN 2002100781

First Edition

Cover: The Mystical Supper
fresco from Vatopaidi Monastery, Mt. Athos
courtesy of Orthodox Byzantine Icons (www.skete.com)

*To those
whose unexpected friendship
inspired these reflections.*

CONTENTS

Introduction...9

1 The Formation of Friendship...15

2 Friendship as Love..29

3 Jonathan and David..41

4 Jesus and His Friends...49

5 Friendship in the Fathers...59

6 A Theology of Friendship..73

7 Friendship in Christian Life..89

8 Issues and Problems in Friendships....................................99

9 Psychological Considerations...121

10 The Feast of Friendship..133

Appendix..145

Bibliography..149

Introduction

"As friendship is a gift we have learned to receive and be immensely grateful for, so we learn through it – and through its ostensible loss – that life itself is a gift" (David Burrell).

If anything is true of life, it is that it is full of surprises – unforeseen twists and turns. One can hardly anticipate what is coming next. So it is with our subject. The roots of this study lie deep within the experience of profound friendships that unexpectedly occurred in my life. They were such that I could never have imagined, let alone anticipated them. Yet because they were so startling and powerful, they begged my deep consideration. What follows is a series of reflections on that experience and on friendship in general from within the tradition of Orthodox Christianity.

Since these friendships completely exceeded the bounds of what I knew friendship to be, at first I had no way of understanding the experience. Although I had some background in psychology as well as philosophy and theology, neither my training nor my previous experience prepared me to comprehend deep friendships of this sort. I had certain direct intuitions about what was happening, but I did not have the conceptual tools to make sense of it at all. So I grappled to achieve some understanding of the process as it unfolded in my life.

While pondering these concerns, I stumbled upon a review of *Love Undetectable* by Andrew Sullivan in *First Things* magazine.[1] The book sounded odd at best, but also intriguing, because it contained a section on friendship that the reviewer granted high praise.

Enlisting the help of a friend and parishioner who is a local bookstore owner, I ordered the book and began to search the available literature on friendship. Surprisingly, not many titles were available. I discovered what nearly every other commentator on the subject of friendship has lamented: it is a subject that suffers near total neglect in contemporary culture.

This is true to some degree of popular literature, but especially of theology, philosophy, psychology, and ethics as well.[2] Gradually, though, I was able to assemble a number of titles on the subject, several of which proved immensely illuminating. I am deeply indebted and stand in awe of authors who became like mentors to me, especially Carolinne White, (St.) Paul Florensky, and Paul Wadell. They are among those who truly *know* the mystery that is friendship. They have made my own experience accessible to myself, and finally, understandable. Thanks are due to them for this inestimable gift.

The purpose of this present work is to unravel the dimensions of a profound personal experience of friendship and to place friendship in the context of an all-embracing theological vision. To do so, I will build on the insights and research of the above authors. My goal is to describe and discuss friendship from within the theological tradition of Orthodox Christianity. I do not intend to be authoritative or dogmatic; "from within" the tradition is an indicator of the framework that surrounds this work. Nor am I attempting to give a comprehensive review of the topic. Thus, I have not discussed at length the views of the various Greek philosophers and schools, which is an immensely important aspect of the subject. Others have covered this ground well, and I see no reason to regurgitate their research and conclusions. I will do so only when it is necessary for the elaboration of this particular account of friendship.

For this task, the work of the incomparable John Zizioulas has been essential. His seminal work, *Being as Communion,* provides the theological framework for my deliberations. As far as I am aware, Paul Florensky is the only Orthodox theologian who has directly considered the theme of friendship theologically. Although certain of his ideas remain controversial to this day, the essential lines of his approach to friendship accord well with Zizoulas' approach to theology, and with his ecclesiology in particular. This is because both men remained fully within the patristic tradition in their understanding of the Church.

Sometime during my early ponderings on the subject, I wrote the essential framework of what is now chapter one. Although it has been revised over and over again, in a sense it stands alone as the record of my initial attempt to philosophically digest the experience. Chapter two reviews some of the basics concerning the nature of friendship love, primarily for those who are unfamiliar with the basic terms of our subject. The next several chapters search out the place of friendship within essential Christian sources, first in the Scriptures and then in the Church Fathers. I have relied on the original research of Carolinne White to document patristic approaches to our topic.

The remaining chapters attempt to place friendship within the essential core of Christian faith and life. I have outlined the basic elements of a theological view of friendship and have sought to demonstrate its importance in Christian life. The study continues with a review of special issues and problems and concludes with a consideration of friendship in relation to eschatology.

I recognize that there is some stylistic inconsistency between various sections. This is due to the varying levels of sophistication necessary to comment on fairly direct biblical accounts, contend with philosophical issues, discuss practical problems, and give an adequate theological account of our subject. I have followed the more modern practice of placing purely bibliographical references in the text, rather than relegating them to footnotes. For the sake of good flow in the text, I have placed discussions of technical issues in the notes, together with references and quotations that have an oblique relationship to the point under discussion. An appendix describes some of the more controversial issues related to the discussion of *philia* in chapter two. I beg the reader's patience and indulgence with regard to the failings and limitations of this book.

Finally, I am thankful to God for the gift of friendship that this study commemorates and celebrates. I am thankful to my friends for the love they have so graciously poured out on me. And lastly, I am thankful to my wife Jeannie for her love and support for over twenty years of marriage and thirty years of friendship. To those of you who mean so much to me, may this in some small way demonstrate my undying love and eternal gratefulness for you.

Notes

1. See *First Things*, vol. 91, March 1999, (60).

2. Following Aristotle, Gilbert Meilaender and Paul Wadell approach friendship within the framework of ethics. Although friendship certainly has serious ethical implications, this might give the impression that it is not a topic to be considered philosophically in its own right, but only as a subset of another subject. Interestingly, there is a body of popular literature on friendship among women written by and for women. See *Girlfriends* (Wildcat Canyon Press, 1995) and other derivative editions by Carmen Renee Berry and Tamara Traeder. In these works, one finds classical friendship themes described in anecdotal fashion. There seems to be no equivalent literature for men, and little for general audiences. There in fact may be some justification to saying that the friendship tradition has been kept alive in literature by women, while nearly disappearing from the experience as well as the literature of men, and languishing as a concern of the culture as a whole.

CHAPTER ONE

The Formation of Friendship

It is snowing outside. As I watch the broad, fat flakes slowly drift toward the ground, the beauty of the scene begins to enrapture me. An emerging elation gradually permeates my soul, but it is a solitary joy that demands to be freed from the confines of its privacy. Intuitively, my heart reaches for a friend. Yet the thought of my friend does not arise after the enchantment begins.[1] It dawns the very moment my soul is drawn into the contemplation of beauty.

Typically, when beauty delights the soul, a person seeks to share the experience. One desires an outlet to communion, someone compatible to share the vision. Watching a gorgeous snowy scene unfold by oneself can at best offer only meager gratification. For the experience to achieve fullness, it must be offered to another in the hope that one's perception, contemplation, and joy will be met, affirmed, and multiplied by the other.[2]

Yet why we yearn to share experience is not immediately obvious. When we consider the matter, some questions come to mind. What is gained by opening one's experience to another? Why share an experience with a particular person? What gives the confidence that another will confirm one's own experience? How does sharing experience lead to the formation of friendship? What characteristics render a person a "friend," with whom one has an ongoing relationship of affinity and affection?

These questions lead to the issue of how friendships originate and develop. Oddly, few of us actively ponder the subject. Most of us have friendships, yet we also tend take the phenomenon of friendship, if not our friends, for granted. We commonly enjoy them without reflecting much on them. Yet when a physical separation occurs in a close friendship, we may feel the absence of our friend quite strongly. When a friendship dissolves because of disagreement or disappointment it can be quite painful. A few moments' reflection is enough for us to realize how important our friendships are to us.

When we think about it, we may not even be able to identify where our friendships begin and end. On one hand, there are family members: parents, children, siblings, other relatives, and spouses. Friendship often is an important element in these relationships. In the case of marriage, for instance, it is pivotal. People often will describe a spouse, sibling, child or parent as a best friend. On the other hand, there are acquaintances. These are people we know and even may have some affection for, but for whom "friend" would be too strong a term. Somewhere in between are friendships that grow out of professional relationships. What separates them from other friendships is that the primary relationship is professional and the friendship secondary.

This study is concerned primarily with friendships that do not involve family members or depend on other principal relationships. These relationships differ from those in that the persons involved *freely choose* to regularly associate with each other *for the mere sake of the other's company*. This is what makes "pure" friendships unique and particularly fascinating. Whereas biological relationship mandates association with family members, romance and desire motivate attraction to lovers and spouses, and business determines professional relationships, pure friendships exist only for themselves. There is no immediately apparent reason why they should even exist.

The Discovery of Friendship

What, then, draws two people together into a friendship? How does a friendship begin? It can only begin with communication. A person shares his observations, ideas, feelings, or humor with another. He extends himself outward toward the other out of regard for him in the confidence that he will understand. Such a self-offering is made in hopes of being reciprocated – although this hope may not even be conscious. *Fear*, however, can thwart this process before it ever gets started. It can prevent potential friendships from forming by causing a person to yield to a perceived threat of rejection. Friendships thus develop when fears and insecurities do not forestall open communication. One person extends himself and the other responds. The pattern begins to repeat itself interchangeably between the partners, and an ongoing dialogue starts to form. Confidence in the conversation grows and fosters the development of trust between the two.

This occurs in different ways with different people. Some individuals naturally seem to have little sense of risk and boldly offer themselves to all comers. The more reticent may find that certain persons elicit confidence from them in way that makes initial communications natural and easy. In any case, the discovery of a certain compatibility fosters a sense of mutuality that becomes progressively stronger over time. However tenuous the initial contacts may have been, the parties find themselves spontaneously and naturally offering thoughts, perceptions, and emotions to the other and gratefully receiving the same. Each person feels fundamentally confirmed by the other. If a true friendship is in the offing, both persons begin to perceive that *something* is there between them. Not only do they simply "like" each other, they sense a "connection" between themselves. They feel a friendship embracing them.

Most friendships take time to develop as trust grows and supports the delicate venture of forming a relationship. However, in some rare cases, friendships spring to life immediately and fully. History supplies a good example in Michel de Montaigne and Etienne La Boetie. Montaigne described it as follows: "At our first meeting, which by chance came at a great feast and gathering in the city, we found ourselves so taken with each other, so well acquainted, so bound together, that from that time nothing was so close to us as each other" (in Pakaluk, 192). The discovery of an immediate friendship like this would be a startling experience for most of us. It certainly is the exception, not the rule.

Honesty and Wholeness in Friendships

There are certain basic requirements for a friendship to thrive. Fundamental honesty is one essential. A friend must be basically honest in order to bring genuine offerings to the relationship. He must have the courage to speak as he knows himself truly to be. This may indeed begin in a limited way, but as a friendship is budding, it progresses to greater fullness. Emerson described it well: "A friend is a person with whom I may be sincere. Before him I think aloud. I am arrived at last at the presence of a man so real and equal that I may drop even those undermost garments of dissimulation, courtesy, and second thought, which men never put off, and may deal with him with the simplicity and wholeness with which one chemical atom meets another" (in Pakaluk, 225).

Even if it is agreed that basic honesty is essential, however, one should not naively assume that there ever can be perfectly pure and uncomplicated motives in friendships. Elements of doubt, insecurity, possessiveness, the need for approval, jealousy, desire for control, sexual desires, defensiveness, projection, dependency and other maladies of the spirit may lie close to the psychological surface of the relationship. Transference can certainly be a powerful factor in friendships. No one is so perceptive as to be aware of the exact nature of all the inner motives operating within him in the conduct of a relationship. Nor, as we shall see, does honesty mean that a totally exhaustive or completely untainted self-disclosure is necessary or even possible. Yet in true friendships, these factors do not definitively cloud the transparency of each soul to the other. They may be issues to some degree for the individuals involved, but they do not impede the growth of the relationship. Its openness is grounded in a basic mutual honesty, which is the source of the communion between the two.

True friendship therefore requires people who are sufficiently whole so as not to be driven by major character deficiencies. Real friendships are never seized by the coercion of neediness; they are discovered in the exercise of free authenticity.[3] Being basically psychologically sound and having a secure sense of self are minimum requirements for the genuine article. When this is the case, the nature of authentic friendship actually may liberate one from limitations rather than providing an opportunity to indulge them. The natural spontaneity of healthy honesty expressed in mutual communion may defuse dysfunctional personal dynamics if they do not dominate the individual friends.

Friendship requires that the parties be basically secure because *naturalness* is one of its most outstanding characteristics. A lack of self-consciousness (which is directly proportional to the intensity of mutual experience) typifies friendships. This allows friends to make profound acts of self-disclosure without hesitation. They are enriched many times over as each receives each other's content, affirms it, and reflects it back through the prism of his own experience. Each one's experience is tested and augmented by the analogous core of the friend's experience and the unique perspectives he brings to bear. Yet despite its depth and power, naturalness is the outstanding characteristic of this process. This naturalness is one element that makes good friendships radiantly joyful and just plain fun.

When this process has taken hold between friends, even disagreements can be experienced as a source of fascination without threatening the bond between their souls. As long as an essential core of mutual values remains in place, individual convictions about many particular issues remain subsidiary to the identity of the relationship itself. Divergent approaches can dwell happily under its lofty canopy of trust and affection.

Friendship and Self

Thus the development of a friendship depends not only on the honest, but the free self-disclosure of each party. Each friend unaffectedly projects his inner self into the center of their common discourse as words, gestures, and other forms of expression, and receives the same from the other. The surprising mutuality of their perceptions reinforces the conviction that the two friends inhabit a realm of shared experience unique to them.

It is an obvious truth, however, that one may never actually experience another person as one experiences oneself. As R.D. Laing puts it, "It is difficult to understand the self-being of *the other*. I cannot experience it directly. I must rely on the other's actions and testimony to infer how he experiences himself" (35, italics his). Yet this brute fact does not dispel in the least the conviction of friends that they participate in a unique and genuine realm of common experience. Above and beyond words and other means of communication, they "know" that they participate in one another. It is an intuitive perception that transcends all the sensory data. As we shall see, this is something that cannot be understood by those outside of it. It is the conversation itself as an ongoing state of communion.

Of course, the reality of shared experience does not exhaust the individual personhood of each friend. Each individual friend retains a mysterious depth of undisclosed personhood that lies underneath the relationship. Even in the most intimate friendships, not all is said. The impossibility of ever fully knowing oneself renders it equally impossible to fully reveal oneself. There are many layers of personhood that necessarily remain undisclosed. Beneath the conversation may lie experiences with family and other friends, some of which are not to be shared, the awareness of unworthy motives in oneself, base and vulgar passions, as well as the perception of one's friend, one's evaluation of how one is perceived, one's wishes as to how to be thought of, and so on. And yet still deeper than these layers of thought, which may be conscious or readily be made conscious, lies the uncharted depths of each person's unconscious motivations and personality structures.[4]

Communion in Friendship

In this light, the circle of shared experience between friends may seem rather small compared to the actual depth of personhood possessed by each friend. Yet genuine friends hardly experience their relationship as shallow or superficial. This is because of their sense that they truly touch each other's souls. What is the source of this conviction?

Interaction between friends consists of a free flow from the depths of each one's soul into the conversation and the reception of the other's content from the conversation into one's own soul. It is important to recognize that the communications are directed into the conversation rather than being simply addressed to the other person because the specific character of those communications is formed by the relationship itself.

The fact that people commonly act in particular ways when with certain other people demonstrates this. The relationship is a mode of being in which both persons participate but which transcends the individuals themselves. The mere coupling of their two sheer personalities does not account for how the *relatedness itself* affects and transforms each of them and thus constitutes its own reality. The relatedness is a creative force that determines the specific characteristics of the persons-in-relation. To put it simply: with friends, it is not just "you plus me" but "you and me as we are when we are together." This shared way of being is experienced as a deepening and broadening of one's individual existence because one partakes of the other's personal reality while also being extended into it and transformed by it.

Robert Spitzer terms this "interpersonal personhood." He writes, "A deep relationship may become a unity, which might be termed 'interpersonal personhood,' in which the connection between two persons takes on a life of its own. Each discovers that a part of his personhood is derived from that connection . . . Deep interpersonal unity becomes a living entity; our *me's* meld into an us" (92, italics his). Neera Badhwar elaborates this point: "A shared history [between friends] can also contribute to the mutual *creation* of characteristics . . . A shared history, in short, both *reveals* and, in part, *constitutes* the object of love" (in Soble, 181, italics hers).

Thus in the conversation of friendship, each friend simultaneously enters the inner sanctuary of the other through the common dimension that exists between them. This dimension then becomes a zone for discovery, not only of the other, but of oneself, as the relationship acts upon each person. The stimulating company of a friend may cause one to see and say things of which one previously had been only dimly aware. The bond of trust and affection formed by mutual experience may elicit what would otherwise be completely unavailable. Thus the relationship itself has a transforming effect on each person. It freshly configures each one's experience in a unique and irreversible way because the nature of the relationship now constitutes each friend.

Qualities of Deep Friendship

These considerations have definitely moved us beyond the sphere of casual friendships to that of "deep" friendships. Such friends have a strong sense that their experience is one. Beyond what we have already discussed, there are several factors that contribute to this. One is found in the distinctiveness of the relationship. As the conversation of friendship grows, it tends to develop its own language and its own "secrets." David Ford describes this phenomenon of "secrecy" between friends as follows: "This need not come from any desire to be exclusive or from deliberate concealment. It is more intrinsic than that. It is simply that the ongoing occurrence of intimacy would have to be participated in to be understood, and that is by definition impossible. What happens in intimacy, whether in twos, or threes, or more, cannot be communicated adequately to those not part of it. It therefore has the character of a secret" (Shape, 107). "Secrecy" therefore concerns not so much particular items that are kept from others, but the unique character of the conversation itself. It is a dialogue that is unlike any other, a world that only these friends inhabit, constituted by the specific qualities of the ways they relate to each other. This can be seen by the private jokes, nicknames, euphemisms, and other peculiarities of their conversation. Such features give a friendship a language all its own, which is necessarily private and inaccessible to outsiders. Of course, others may be admitted as the friends determine.

In very deep friendships, the friends often have the sense

that their friend actually dwells in them. Theologian David Ford describes this phenomenon as the "community of the heart." He writes, "These are the people who indwell us, who are at the core of our 'home life' as a self. We always live in their presence, whether they are physically there or not" (Shape, 32). Thus, good friends will often converse with the other by imagination when apart. In such imaginary encounters they review their shared memories and develop ideas for pursuit in the future. They sense that they are incorporated into each other. Ford observes, "They are inside us as well as outside us. They may be on the other side of the world, or they may be dead, but they are constantly before us and within us. They are so deep within us that we can never come to terms in any final way – we can never get them 'into perspective'" (Shape, 32-33).

This deep form of connection sometimes manifests itself in sudden and dramatic ways. Friends discover that they had set out to contact each other with an unpredictable yet identical idea in mind. Although separated by lengthy periods and many miles, they discover each other to be reading the same literature, absorbed in similar contemplations, grappling with common problems, engaging in similar activities, even buying the same products. In some cases, the conversation becomes so profound that it occurs without words and beyond emotions. The achievement of such an unforeseeable understanding then is a source of profound joy and deep affection. It gives close friends the deep sense of sharing the same soul.[5]

One writer has described her experience of such deep friendships as follows: "There is another kind of friend that transcends the social friend and I have only had a few grace my life. These few are burned into my soul with a love I cannot put into words . . . The extraordinary qualities of these rare friendships are the communication that takes place between the individuals and the feeling that these friendships are more than chance meetings. There are no barriers to overcome: when something is said, it is immediately understood. A wonderful spark is present in these friendships . . . I imagine this is the type of friendship Aristotle had in mind when he wrote these words: 'What is a friend? A single soul in two bodies.'"[6]

Conclusion

A friend is one with whom the reality of shared experience becomes ongoing and continuous for us. He is one to whom we turn naturally and unselfconsciously when we are struck by the most meaningful moments of life – heightened experiences of perception, insight, and feeling - but also to share the mundane details of our days. The qualities of our individual experience are expanded, enhanced, enriched and recast in the context of our conversation with him. The enjoyment of each other's company becomes personal tradition and trust fully flowers in the embrace of the relationship. Opening ourselves to one another, we come to share a common realm that is unique to us and greater than the sum of our individualities.

These observations on the origination, development, and ultimate shape of our friendships reveal the profound meaning that friendships have in our lives. However, we have not discussed the nature of the bond that friends experience between themselves, nor have we sought to closely distinguish friendship from other types of treasured human relationships. It is to these considerations that we now turn.

1 Notes

1. Sometime after writing these first lines, I noted that Paul Florensky also began his discussion of friendship in the contemplation of falling snow and the thought of a friend: "The snowstorm swirls in endless circles, covering the window with a fine snowy ash and beating against the window glass . . . Let the window be covered by the snow. It's good when that happens. The lamp inside burns more brightly; the incense is more fragrant, the flame of the fragrant candle is more even. Again I am with you. Every day I remember something about you, and then I sit down to write" (284-5).

2. Francis Bacon observes, "[T]his communicating of a man's self to his friend works two contrary effects; for it redoubleth joys, and cutteth griefs in halves. For there is no man, that imparteth his joys to his friend, but he joyeth the more; and no man, that imparteth his griefs to his friend, but he grieveth the less" (in Pakaluk, 204). Just before his tragic death by starvation in the Alaskan bush at age 24, the lone adventurer Chris McCandless ruefully drew the following conclusion: "And so it turned out that only a life similar to those around us, merging with it without a ripple, is genuine life, and that an unshared happiness is not happiness . . . and this was most vexing of all: HAPPINESS (IS) ONLY REAL WHEN SHARED." (Krakauer, 189, capitals his). However, an Orthodox bishop once told me what an older archimandrite once said to him: "One can be sure of a vocation to celibacy when one sees something beautiful, and feels no need to share the experience with someone else."

3. Emerson writes, "Our friendships hurry to short and poor conclusions, because we have made them a texture of wine and dreams, instead of the tough fibre of the human heart. The laws of friendship are austere and eternal, of one web with the laws of nature and of morals . . . We seek our friend not sacredly, but with an adulterate passion which would appropriate him to ourselves. In vain. We are armed all over with subtle antagonisms, which, as soon as we meet, begin to play, and translate all poetry into stale prose" (in Pakaluk, 224).

4. Although the entire bulk of *Self and Others* deals with these problems, Laing pays special attention to the problem of "collusion," when two individuals cooperate to foist false identities on each other in a relationship. This involves the complex interactions between one's own self-concept, the self-concept of the other, the perceptions each one has of the other, and the persons as they really are. See his discussion (108-111).

5. For anecdotal descriptions in the experiences of women friends, see Carmen Renee Berry and Tamara Traeder, *TrueBlue Friends*, (Andrews McMeel Publishing, Kansas City, MO, 2000), particularly the chapter entitled "Soul Connections."

6. Jonopoulos (85).

Chapter Two

Friendship as Love

The subject of "love" certainly is not suffering neglect in modern Western society. It is highlighted in every form of popular media. For instance, few things are given more attention in popular culture than the notion of "falling in love." We frequently hear the word "love" in many familiar but different contexts. We understand it when a wife tells her husband that she "does not love him anymore" in a TV drama. The meaning is clear when a high school girl tells a friend she has fallen in love with a boy in her class. When a mother tells her four year-old daughter how much she loves her, we know what she means. If a young man enthusiastically informs a friend how much he loves his new set of golf clubs, we get the point. When Jesus commands us to love our neighbor as ourselves, there is little mystery as to what he asks.

In recognizing distinct senses of the word "love" in these different contexts, we realize that this one word can carry some very diverse connotations. We grasp that it can refer to sexual desire, the warmth of affection, charitable acts and dispositions, a high degree of regard and appreciation, or a burning devotion to another person. All these meanings and more are covered by the one English word "love."

Friendship and the Forms of Love

The use of the word "love" with regard to friendship is not very common in modern American culture, but it is not unknown. We can easily imagine a woman telling a close friend she loves her. It is harder to imagine the same between two men. The notion that friends are in a relationship of love in fact may sound strange to some.

The same would not have been true for the ancient Greeks. Whereas in modern English the one word "love" has a wide range of meanings, classical Greek contains four distinct terms for love. Although there is some overlap in their usage, they have reasonably identifiable definitions.[1] *Eros* is the love that is desire, a desire for union with the object of one's affections. Oftentimes, it is defined as sexual desire, but this is to reduce its rich and full content to just one of its possible forms. Sexual desire is indeed a form of *eros*, but not all *eros* is sexual desire. The Fathers of the Church speak of God's *eros* for his creatures, and the *eros* of the soul for union with God.[2] Eros is a passionate yearning for union whose most familiar image is the longing of a man and woman for each other.

Storge is translated by C.S. Lewis as "affection."[3] It is that warm, pleasant, and cozy feeling perhaps best expressed in the love grandparents have for their grandchildren, or that of children for pets. It is characterized by peace rather than passion, by comfort rather than desire. It cuddles and caresses, wanting to be close for the sake of closeness and nothing more. Paul Florensky describes it as "*a calm and permanent feeling in the depths of the loving one*" (287, italics his). It is the experience of closeness and warmth with another for its own sake, without any forethought, agenda, or ulterior motive.

Agape is the form of love most celebrated in the New Testament and the Christian tradition. It is the self-sacrificing love that places the other before self. It seeks to serve the ultimate well-being of another regardless of cost to self. *Agape* takes no account of the relative value, worth, or deserts of another person precisely because it assigns supreme value and worth to every person. It is not only a favorable disposition toward others, but is action based on the same. It is a form of love that comes from God, even as it is characteristic of God. It was absolutely realized in Jesus Christ; he is its perfect image.

The ancient Greeks also counted friendship as a form of love. Their word for it was *philia*. *Philia* was for them one of the noblest achievements of human nature. It bore an essential relationship to the good and virtuous life. C.S. Lewis put it this way: "To the Ancients, Friendship seemed the happiest and most fully human of all loves; the crown of life and the school of virtue. The modern world, in comparison, ignores it" (87). Earlier he states, "[V]ery few modern people think Friendship a love of comparable value or even a love at all" (87).

Most modern writers (among the few who have actually taken up the subject) have lamented the modern neglect of friendship as a topic for inquiry and investigation.[4] Yet friendship is foundational to most of our lives. Why this neglect? Lewis is probably correct when he asserts that many no longer recognize friendship as a true form of love. I propose that there are two basic reasons for this. First, friendship literally does not have "sex appeal." We live in a society that exalts erotic love as the supreme fulfillment available to human beings. How can friendship compete with the sizzle of sex in the arena of public attention? The other reason is that friendship does not offer the immediate moral appeal of *agape*. We thus understand the fascination that people had with the love life of Princess Diana and the charitable work of Mother Theresa. In one memorable week of 1998, *eros* and *agape* both received astounding public homage. But who can recall a public celebration of friendship?

Yet only a little reflection is sufficient to establish that friendship is indeed a form of love. First of all, a friend is valued and appreciated. This is in keeping with the most basic use of the word "love," as when we say that we "love" certain things, including inanimate objects. We "love" them because we value and appreciate particular qualities they possess. Yet the love we have for a friend obviously is much more than this. We hold a friend in especially high regard; we respect and esteem his *person*. We find that we singularly treasure his unique and unrepeatable configuration of human personhood. Thus we develop great *affection* for him. We *feel* a certain way about a friend. This affection that grows out of respect and esteem is definitely a form of love.

Because of our esteem and affection for our friend, we *desire* his company. If there is an "erotic" component to friendship it is not primarily sexual, but this. We enjoy being with him. We think of him fondly and look forward to opportunities to be with him. We love our friend. No other word will do it justice.

Finally, our love for a friend gives birth to commitment. As discussed above, we find that we share various values, perceptions and interests with a friend. This experience of mutuality causes us to be committed to the friend himself, and not just the things we share in common with him. Because of our commitment, we are devoted to the well-being of our friend in everything. We are ready to sacrifice of ourselves for the sake of our friend. At this point in our relationship, *philia* has embraced *agape*. The love of friendship is complete.

Expressions of Friendship

There is little question, then, that friendship must be understood as a form of love. It embraces the essential qualities of love from the rudimentary to the exalted. Why then, we might ask, is this not widely recognized? Why are there so few expressions of this love in art and culture? Why is the love that is friendship not generally celebrated?

We may not be able to answer these questions.[5] But we can say that it has not always been so. In other epochs, *philia* was given vibrant expression. Let us turn to some examples.

St. Augustine characterized the love of a departed friend as "sweeter than all the pleasures of life" (in White, 186). Such language from a man about another man in modern Western culture would likely cause much nervousness as well as misunderstanding. Yet it was not at all atypical of the patristic era. Speaking of friendship in such warm phraseology in fact hearkens back to the Old Testament where, as we shall see, in ancient Israel, David uses similar language concerning Jonathan. In the medieval West, Aelred of Rievaulx speaks of Christ as the inspiration of one's love for a friend, ". . . so that charm may follow upon charm, sweetness upon sweetness and affection upon affection. And thus, friend cleaving to friend in the spirit of Christ, is made with Christ but one heart and one soul, and so mounting aloft through degrees of love to friendship with Christ, he is made one spirit with him in one kiss" (in Wadell, 108). Although the love of Christ is mystically intertwined here with the love of one's earthly friend, it is apparent that the delicate affections of friendship are not merely those of the soul with Christ but exist between the souls of friends who are joined in Christ. What is striking, then, are not the typically medieval expressions of spiritual union but the celebration of the sweetness of friendship in Christ.

As we move toward the modern period, we find examples of the appreciation of friendship that are certainly less mystical and Christ-centered but nonetheless still show it as a most powerful affection. Montaigne is a case in point: "In the friendship I speak of, our souls mingle and blend with each other so completely they efface the seam that joined them and cannot find it again . . . I know not what quintessence of all this mixture, which, having seized his whole will, led it to plunge and lose itself in mine, with equal hunger . . ." (in Pakaluk,193). Andrew Sullivan points out that it would be easy to conclude that Montaigne was here describing an erotic relationship.[6] Yet Montaigne is absolutely clear that he is not; in fact, he pointedly disdains *eros* in favor of the intense *philia* he describes.[7] But for our purposes, it is noteworthy how passionate his approach to friendship is. Again, to feel such intense love for friends is, if not unknown, at least highly suspect in contemporary Western culture.

Other examples could certainly be drawn. But the point has been established. We live in an era that has a deeply impoverished appreciation for friendship. In contrast to previous epochs, we barely recognize that it is a genuine form of love that is to be lived out passionately and expressed boldly. Our all-pervasive preoccupation with sexuality leaves little room for *philia* to be celebrated and praised. The purpose of this present work is to promote the rediscovery of friendship in all its human richness and divine significance. Having done so, hopefully we then will be able to take our place among the wise of all ages that have lived and rejoiced in this distinctive and beautiful form of love.

Types of Friendship

Before we can advance this agenda, however, we must first clarify our understanding of what friendship is. To be sure, it is a particular sort of relationship. But there is not simply one kind of relationship that we call "friendship." One size does not fit all. There must be as great a variety of styles of friendship as there are varieties of unique personalities. Nevertheless, like everything else in life, there are certainly broad categories or types of friendship that account for the dominant features of most such relationships. Although people may use the term "friendship" to cover wildly diverse situations, there yet remains a definite core content that would indicate to most that a relationship is indeed a "friendship." We may not be able to give it a brief and easy definition, but it is a phenomenon that most people can readily identify.

The concept of friendship as we know it originated among the ancient Greeks, having developed from earlier more functional forms of camaraderie. By the time of Aristotle, it was a subject of considerable reflection. He devoted the 8th and 9th books of his Nicomachean Ethics to discussing it. In this work, Aristotle gave the classic exposition of the types of friendship, and his thought on the topic has remained a standard exposition to this day. Undoubtedly, there has been a lack of sustained modern philosophical inquiry into the issue, which has left the classical masters still firmly in control of the matter. We thus now turn to some of the basic ideas of the ancient philosophers for the insights that ground friendship among the supreme forms of love.

Aristotle described three main categories of friendship.[8] They are friendships of *usefulness, pleasure,* and *virtue.* In friendships of *usefulness,* a compatible relationship builds itself on absorption in a common task, or because one party is providing a valuable service to the other. A sense of esteem and comradery emerge, but the development of affection and mutuality is stymied by a failure to transcend the functional nature of the relationship. For instance, two people are engaged in work together on a volunteer committee. During the time of their service together, they are in frequent communication about their work. They find their contacts with each other gratifying and pleasurable. A relationship begins to build around their committee work. However, when their terms of service on the committee are over, contacts between the two fade away. Basically, the relationship ends because it consisted of their usefulness to each other for the commission of certain tasks. When that work is over, so is the "friendship."

Friendships of *pleasure* comprise the vast majority of friendships. Despite the hedonistic ring that this title has, there is nothing inherently morally faulty about them. We enter this type of friendship because we find another person pleasant to be with. We enjoy his sense of humor, find his conversation stimulating, share similar interests in certain pursuits, or like to engage in the same activities. The pleasure we derive from his company is reason enough for the friendship. We like being around him. An example would be a friendship between two men who are baseball fans. Each finds the other's personality basically agreeable, and they share a passion for their favorite sport. Thus they attend games together, swap memorabilia, discuss the performance of star players, enjoy monitoring a wide variety of baseball statistics, and drink beer together. They are great "buddies." As time goes on, a sense of commitment and loyalty may develop between them, which causes them to be deeply solicitous for each other's welfare. But the enjoyment of each other's company remains the foundation of the relationship.

Among women, a friendship of pleasure may have a more deeply personal character. Rather than focusing on common interests and activities, women often focus on the content of their lives and their emotional states. But although the relationship may have a depth lacking in many male friendships, the same pleasure principle still applies: The most important aspect of the relationship for each person is what she gets out of it. In other words, the other is esteemed because "she makes me feel good." The pleasurable feelings one derives from the relationship are its reason for being. Again, a deep mutual commitment may arise from this, but at the core remains a devotion to the enjoyment provided by the friend.

The final and most important type of friendship is a friendship of virtue. It seems that this type of friendship is rare in our day; indeed, it may have been rare in Aristotle's day. In these friendships, the friends are attracted by the good they see in each other. The common dedication to virtue and high ideals brings them together. In the words of Paul Wadell, "In virtue friendships, each loves the other for his or her own sake because each loves the good, and the friend, to some degree embodies the good; in short, they love one another because they are virtuous" (52).

We can see here that virtue friendships are constituted by a transcendent principle, the good. Yet paradoxically, the devotion of the friends to an ideal that transcends them causes each to be devoted to the person of the other. This is because the good and the virtuous are only seen and known as they are embodied in other persons. Thus virtue friendships simultaneously produce dedication to transcendent values and intense devotion to the friend.

An example of virtue friendships can be found in monastic life. Imagine a pair of monks who share an equal devotion to the attainment of virtue and union with God. Each one finds the other to be in some respects an exemplar of the virtues he seeks to attain. The devotion of each is energized by the encounter with the other who represents in many ways the very thing he yearns and strives for, and yet who is unquestionably a companion on the journey. In terms of usefulness or pleasure, the relationship has little to offer. But when it comes to spiritual growth and the attainment of godliness, each recognizes that the friendship holds forth untold possibilities. Because of this, their love for each other is unbounded. It partakes of eternity. Resting not only in the limited capacities of fallible men, it shares in divine ideals that transcend all time and historical circumstance.

From the Human to the Divine

Gilbert Meilander notes how Plato recognized that friendships have the potential to elevate persons from the merely human to the realm of the divine. According to Meilaender, Plato saw that preferential friendships have value insofar as they are a means to participating in a "universally shared love" (12). The threat in Platonic thought is that the particular friend will ultimately "disappear" in the contemplation of the universal goodness, love, and beauty that he leads us to. But the impact of Plato's view, according to Meilaender, is that friendship must "lead beyond itself . . . when it is believed to be an image of and preparation for some greater love in a greater and more universal community" (16).

What may appear as a threat is also friendship's great promise. Friendship is an image and intimation of a love greater than itself, which need not negate or relativize the actual personal relationship. Rather the friendship is an icon, a window, into a greater, broader communion of love. This communion encompasses every authentic friendship but cannot itself be encompassed by any one of them.

We have considered how friendship is a true form of love, and that when it reaches its highest realization, it is a pathway to a love that is universal and divine. It is now time to turn our attention to the Christian tradition to see how this insight has been developed in the life of the Church of Christ.

THE FEAST OF FRIENDSHIP

2 Notes

1. There are several studies that explore the meaning of these four Greek terms. C.S. Lewis' classic study *The Four Loves* is a good introduction, although it is not a work of philology and tends to overdraw the distinction between the terms. Anders Nygren's *Eros and Agape* discusses those two terms from an evangelical (Lutheran) Christian perspective and describes them as two opposing principles. Paul Florensky gives a good introduction to the four forms in the chapter on Friendship in his *Pillar and Ground of Truth* (286-293). A more recent compendium is Alan Soble's *Eros, Agape and Philia.*

2. Orthodox theology sees God's love as a unitive force, because God desires to unite himself to man in order to pour out his boundless plenitude upon him throughout eternity. Thus, the Divine love for man is "erosic" from it deepest origin. It manifests itself as agapic in so far as it continues to be extended to man in spite of his rebellion, sin, and subjection to death. Likewise the erotic power in man represents his yearning for the divine. (See George Capsanis, *The Eros of Repentance,* 1-4).

3. Lewis' third chapter on "storge'" is titled "Affection," and he translates the Greek word consistently as such.

4. On this point, see Lewis, 87, Sullivan, 176-7, Meilaender, 1-3, Pakaluk, vii.

5. Andrew Sullivan holds that fear of homosexuality limits male to male expressions fellowship and intimacy, thus causing friendship as a whole to be underrated in our society (see 234-5).

6. "Indeed, at times, in this case, it is hard to avoid the conclu-

sion that Montaigne was in love with his friend . . . Except, of course, that Montaigne is quite clear that he had no physical attraction to Le Boetie and didn't consummate his friendship sexually. It existed rather as a platonic longing so intense that we have almost forgotten how to achieve it today" (228).

7. See Montaigne's lengthy comparison of the two, in Pakaluk, 189-191).

8. See his Nicomachean Ethics, book 8:3, (in Pakaluk, 32-6).

CHAPTER THREE

Jonathan and David

There are those who hold that *philia*, the love of friends, is a phenomenon not given much attention in the Bible. Rather than being a biblical, Hebraic concern, it is commonly held to be a typically classical Greek preoccupation. There is no question that ancient Greek philosophers treated the subject systematically and at length. Yet although *philia* is not discussed systematically in the Scriptures, its presence is found quite readily in several important biblical narratives. One of the most important is the story of Jonathan and David found in the book of 1 Samuel. Let us consider this unusual story.

"And it came to pass, when he [David] had made an end of speaking to Saul, that the soul of Jonathan was knit with the soul of David, and Jonathan loved him as his own soul . . . Then Jonathan and David made a covenant, because he loved him as his own soul. And Jonathan stripped himself of the robe which was upon him, and gave it to David, and his garments, even to his sword, and to his bow, and to his girdle" (1 Sam. 18:1, 3-4).

A number of important topics surface in this, the beginning of the account. First, we may note the suddenness of the connection between Jonathan and David, similar to what we have observed in Montaigne. Again, although it shares some similarities, this is not an example of "falling in love." We have seen that the tendency to eroticize every form of attraction and deep connection between human beings is an unfortunate symptom of the modern American fixation on sexuality. It reflects a cultural environment that exalts *eros* and has lost much sense of the meaning of *philia*. Minds formed in such cultural impoverishment cannot help but misinterpret the love between Jonathan and David because they understand little of love outside the erotic context.[1]

Friendships Sudden and Gradual

Although the notion of "falling in love" carries inherent erotic connotations in this culture, a sudden but pure occurrence of *philia* may share other of its characteristics. As discussed above, two individuals sense immediately upon meeting one another – or discover soon thereafter – a powerful affinity of spirit between them. The reasons for this may vary. Usually there is the sense that the new acquaintance shares fundamental commonalities with oneself. Surprise and joy burst forth in the soul as one discovers that the other's experience is "just like mine," that he holds identical views, loves the same activities, or completely shares a particular perspective. With time, the new friends find this initial experience of commonality broadening and deepening.[2]

In other cases, perhaps, the initial attraction may be based on the perception that other possesses qualities, insights, or perspectives lacking in oneself. Thus individuals may find themselves attracted to those who seem to be their opposite. As long as they have enough in common to facilitate understanding, such original experiences of differing perspectives can be fascinating and attractive. If a good friendship springs to life from them, these divergences may end up being sources of great enrichment, opening up realms of experience that had been previously inaccessible for each friend. This serves to make such friendships deeply satisfying.

Another example of a way a fast friendship can materialize is when individuals share a compatible sense of humor. A bond quickly develops between them because of mutual amusement and shared laughter. There is doubtless a multitude of ways in which a person may find another immediately likable and from which a friendship quickly blossoms.

The difference, however, between such sudden occurrences of *philia* and "falling in love" is the absence of yearning and desire in the first. In an erotic connection, the couple feels a passionate yearning to complete the relationship physically. Without sexual fulfillment, the relationship feels incomplete and frustrating. The exact opposite is true in the formation of a friendship. The relationship is already complete. It simply must be revealed as such, and this may happen quickly or take some time. When it occurs, whether quickly or slowly, there is no sense of being possessed by desire and yearning. Rather, there is the peace of knowing another as one's own soul. This is what we see in the story of Jonathan and David. Their friendship is simply revealed. From the very beginning it is complete and whole and yearning for other types of completion have no place in it.

We have seen that not every good friendship begins with a sudden, unexpected connection. Most build much more slowly over time.[3]   Initial contacts may not be especially noteworthy. They offer little indication of common perspectives or mutual vision. Yet as time passes, chance conversations develop into an ongoing dialogue, which begins to manifest the fundamental elements that catalyze friendship. The realization dawns on each sooner or later that "we are becoming good friends." This pathway to friendship is analogous to the situation where long-time acquaintances discover themselves gradually "falling in love."

The case of Jonathan and David thus represents an example of the immediate occurrence of philia between two individuals. The result of the bond between them was that "the soul of Jonathan was knit with the soul of David," the essential characteristic of deep friendship that we have discussed above. It is therefore clear that the Scriptures recognize this elemental human experience. Christians thus cannot help but believe that this example is enshrined in the Bible as God's witness to the blessedness of *philia*. The account is hardly arbitrary or incidental. It is a revelation.

Generosity and Loyalty

The deep friendship of Jonathan and David causes them to experience their souls as one. It also immediately motivates Jonathan to give David his garments and armaments. As the story develops, we find Jonathan risking the wrath of his father and even his own life for David's sake (see 1 Sam. 20: 25-34). These actions point up two characteristics of intense *philia*: generosity and loyalty. Jonathan's gifts of his garments and arms are more than just a gesture of "niceness" to a new friend. Still less is he trying to buy David's friendship. David, the young shepherd, was indeed rough and needy, certainly without the garb and arms that a king's son would possess. Yet Jonathan is not offering him charity. His generosity reflects the drive of a friend to share his bounty with his friend. In other words, when friendship is real and deep, it is typical for one to wish to share his every good with the one he loves. One seeks to express one's affection in tangible ways, to act kindly solely for the sake of bringing joy and blessing to the friend.

The loyalty of Jonathan to David is rightly the stuff of legend. It was no small matter in ancient Near Eastern culture to deceive one's father and act contrary to his wishes. Yet Jonathan readily does so for David's sake, recognizing, of course, the injustice of his father's jealousy of David. The biblical account, however, reveals that the bond of communion between two friends is such that no external force can rupture it. There is one internal phenomenon that can: betrayal.

Betrayal occurs when one of the parties, for whatever reason, turns away from the communion that gave birth to the friendship. It may be an abandonment of shared faith, an act against mutual moral commitments, a transgression against an esteemed value or principle, or even a hostile act toward the other. In any case, the act is such that a fundamental supporting element of their unity has been destroyed, and continuation of the friendship is no longer possible. Loyalty to the common vision is essential to the perpetuation of friendship. Jonathan reveals this virtue of genuine *philia*.

Philia as a Pathway to Divinity

The completeness of Jonathan's loyalty to David is shown by the fact that he is even willing to forgo his rights to his father's throne and give them to his friend. This only can be explained, I believe, by the notion that Jonathan perceived divine destiny at work in David. Their common oath reveals that their communion in friendship was grounded in God: "The Lord be between you and me forever" (1 Sam. 20:23). The shared element that unites their souls is not merely human affection. It is a *philia* that has transcended itself into divine communion. It is not just their love, but the Lord who is between them. This is the first biblical indication that *philia* itself can be an opening to the presence of God.

Jonathan is therefore able to lay aside his own prerogatives for his friend because the relationship has opened him to divine vision. His communion with his friend has become a pathway to divine illumination.

The great intensity of *philia* between these two men of God is expressed by David's lament for the slain Jonathan: "I am distressed for thee, my brother Jonathan; very pleasant has thou been to me; thy love to me was wonderful, surpassing the love of women" (2 Sam. 1:26). It is difficult to describe how amazing, how stunning this statement truly is. That David, certainly no stranger to the wonders of *eros*, would describe his *philia* for Jonathan as "surpassing the love of women" is simply astounding. It is no less than an awe-inspiring, eye-opening revelation of the true power of *philia* to enrapture a person into a state of communion beyond that possible of sexual love.

The story of the blossoming of friendship between Jonathan and David reveals *philia* as a human phenomenon capable of bearing divinity. As an initiation into one of the most profound forms of love, friendship can engender an intensity that stimulates the highest achievements of loyalty and devotion possible for human beings.

3 Notes

1. Discussing modern confusion regarding friendship, William Lynch points to the unhelpful influence of Freud: "Unfortunately we have been further hindered here by Freud's doctrine that affection and tenderness are really forms of defeated sexuality; here is a good example of the need to examine every concrete, clinical suggestion on its own merits. For one thing, we should be aware that Freud himself was no great genius at either friendship or collaboration" (41-2).

2. As Andrew Sullivan puts it, "Friendship can only really be experienced when both friends are fully used to each other . . . friendship draws strength from the past, from myriad shared jokes and understandings, from the remembrance of moments endured or celebrated together . . ." (203-4).

3. For Emerson, this is the norm and he repeatedly emphasizes it: "Let us buy our entrance to this guild by a long probation. Why should we desecrate noble and beautiful souls by intruding on them? Why insist on rash personal relations with your friend? . . . Respect so far the holy laws of this fellowship as to not prejudice its perfect flower by your impatience for its opening" (229-30). Andrew Sullivan agrees: "Where love is swift, for example, friendship is slow. Love comes quickly, as the song has it, but friendship ripens with time . . . we don't 'fall in friendship'" (202-3).

CHAPTER FOUR

Jesus and His Friends

The strong emphasis on divine love in the Gospel of John has earned it the nickname of "the Gospel of love." John's dramatic presentation of God as love is one of the highest summits of New Testament theology. In the Eastern Church, the author of the fourth gospel is most commonly referred to as "John the Theologian" because of his distinctive interpretation of Jesus as the incarnate Logos of God who becomes flesh out of love for fallen mankind.

An additional title for this Gospel might indeed be "the Gospel of friendship." John's Gospel presents Jesus particularly in the role of friend. In fact, if the traditional identification of the "disciple whom Jesus loved" as this Gospel's source is accurate, its emphasis on friendship actually may be based on the unique friendship between Jesus and this disciple.

Lazarus, Martha, and Mary

A good place to observe John's accentuation of friendship unfold is the story of the raising of Lazarus in chapter 11. We will not recount the entire story here, but rather isolate those passages that relate to friendship in particular.

At the beginning of the account, Jesus receives news that Lazarus is ill. The message comes from his sisters as follows: "He whom you love is sick" (11:3). After recounting this, the evangelist adds this qualifying remark: "Now Jesus loved

Martha and her sister and Lazarus" (11:5). There are several elements in this short verse that are worthy of comment.

First, we may note Jesus' love of Martha, Mary (the sister) and Lazarus. It is common for pious Christians to discourse about the love of Jesus; usually the focus is on the love that Jesus has for every human person. The underlying assumption behind such pious rhetoric is that Jesus loves each person equally. But Jesus did not love Martha, Mary, and Lazarus in the same sense that he loved "everyone." That is not the point here. Rather, the evangelist is highlighting the exact opposite: Jesus had a special love for Martha, Mary, and Lazarus.

This fact has a direct bearing on an issue that has plagued much of the Western Christian discussion of friendship ethics. There have been a number of theologians who have objected to the notion that *philia* can be a Christian affection.[1] They have asserted that agape is the distinctive Christian expression of love, and that it is fundamentally opposed to *philia*. This is because *philia* is by nature preferential, while the Christian ideal is that love be offered equally to all. Yet this idealistic contention runs up against the example of the Master, who clearly indulged in a number of preferential relationships. Not only did Jesus have a special affection for Martha, Mary, and Lazarus, but among his disciples, one clearly stood out as "the disciple whom Jesus loved."[2] Those who wish to malign engagement in preferential friendships as an unchristian practice are seeking to place themselves on a higher ethical plane than the Lord himself.

The fact of the matter is that Jesus had friends. He had disciples, followers, and to be sure, many acquaintances. Yet among those he numbered a few as friends. Friendship as a special preferential relationship thus has the inherent endorsement of the Lord himself who actively participated in such relationships. Nor should this observation strike us as being particularly unusual. A careful student of the Scriptures will be aware that in every epoch, God himself has special friends. From Noah to Abraham to Moses to David and beyond, there are a number of biblical characters that, for whatever reason, enjoy the special favor of God.

One of the most striking aspects of the story, as I read it, is the fact that Jesus is said to have loved not only Lazarus, but Martha and Mary as well. It is one thing to recognize that Jesus had special friendships with other men. It is of great importance, however, to note that he also counted these two women as his friends. If preferential friendships in general have been a problem for some Christians, cross-gender friendships present a veritable hornet's nest of problems. Undoubtedly, there are many issues involved in the consideration of whether or not such friendships are advisable. There are the obvious potential pitfalls, and we will consider these issues later on. However, at this point, it is valuable just to take note that the Lord himself had the same special love for Martha and Mary as he did for their brother.

Why did Jesus have this special love for Lazarus, Martha, and Mary? Were they especially kind, generous, or hospitable with him? Was it their virtue or receptivity to his teaching? We don't know. The Gospel does not give us any reasons for Jesus' special love for them. It only states and portrays the fact of his love. So any further comment on the question would be pure speculation and conjecture. We can safely assume only one thing: Jesus was fond of them. He enjoyed their company. He liked to spend time with them. And so it is natural for Christians to do the same; they will spend time freely with those they especially enjoy.

As the narrative continues, Jesus decides it is time to go to Lazarus. He communicates this to the disciples as follows: "Our friend Lazarus sleeps, but I go to wake him" (11:11). Here he clearly identifies Lazarus as he has yet done with none other: Lazarus is his friend, and the friend of the disciples. When he arrives at the tomb, the power of his love becomes clear. Jesus stands at his grave and weeps, and the depth of his feeling for Lazarus stuns the bystanders. "See how he loved him!" they remark (11:36). Although it has become traditional to conceive Jesus' weeping at Lazarus tomb as a general lament for the fate of humanity subject to death, the narrative makes it clear that it was the intensity of his particular love for Lazarus that impressed those who watched him.

Thus it is clear that Jesus manifested an intense, devoted, unique and particular affection for Lazarus. Lazarus was his friend. His relationship to him was unlike his relationship with others. There was a special bond between them. The thought of the cessation of that friendship on account of death brought forth an ardent outpouring of grief from Jesus: "See how he loved him!" Friendships were a passionate matter for the Lord.

The Beloved Disciple

Jesus' affinity with "the disciple whom he loved" (see Jn. 13:23, 19:26, 21:7, 20) demonstrates this more fully. This disciple is singled out from all the others as having a uniquely close relationship with Jesus. The relationship is only mentioned in the Gospel of John, and the disciple is never named. The traditional inference is that John was indeed that disciple, and the tradition stemming from him does not name him out of humility and reticence.

The intimacy of their friendship is demonstrated by the first occasion where this disciple is identified as such. He was the one who reclined "at the Lord's breast" at the Last Supper (see 13:23). The image is particularly striking to those of Western culture, even though most of us have observed it in portraits of the Last Supper. The physical closeness between Jesus and this disciple is a manifestation of the closeness of their hearts. What was it about this particular disciple that Jesus so loved? It may have been his purity, his honesty, his courage, his spiritual understanding, his commitment to him, or any number of other characteristics. We are not told. What is apparent is that there was a deep compatibility between his heart and that of Jesus.

This truth demonstrates the fact that certain persons will be naturally drawn to other persons by a fundamental kinship of spirit. The result will be the formation of a preferential relationship between them. They will experience a closeness that few, if any, others will be able to share. Such friends may not readily understand what is occurring between them at first. It is an intuitive connection between hearts that may be unexpected or outwardly unlikely. Yet its depth and power are undeniable from the outset.

The intensity of the beloved disciple's reciprocal love is revealed by the fact that he alone among all the disciples stood by Jesus during his abject humiliation on the cross. Along with his mother and the other women, the beloved disciple showed unflinching loyalty by his attention to Jesus' passion (see 19:25-7). His connection to Jesus is unsurpassed, and that is why he is entrusted with the care of his mother. Jesus evidently felt that he above all others would have the heart for his mother that would most closely approximate his own. Of course, this is because Jesus already knows the sinews of his beloved's heart to be inextricably intertwined with his.

The Disciples as Friends

It would be a mistake, however, to conclude that the intensity of Jesus' love for this disciple translated into exclusivity. One of the crowning moments in Jesus' relationship with his disciples is when he specifically recognizes all of them as no longer servants, but as friends. "Greater love has no one than this, than to lay down his life for his friends. You are my friends if you do whatever I command you. No longer do I call you servants, for a servant does not know what his master is doing; but I have called you friends, for all things that I have heard from my Father I have made known to you" (Jn. 15:13-15).

There are several features of this passage that are worthy of consideration. First, Jesus' insistence that giving one's life for one's friends is the highest form of love is somewhat surprising, given his emphasis on loving enemies and giving sacrificially to the undeserving. In other words, one might conclude on the basis of his teaching elsewhere that it would be a higher act to sacrifice one's life for those who do not deserve it. But no, Jesus here clearly identifies giving one's life for one's friends as the highest possible form of love. Why?

Perhaps it is because giving one's life for a friend is an act of love that is formed and carried out within the communion of love. Giving one's life for a stranger might be heroic and valiant, but it does not arise from the bosom of love as such would for a friend. There is no "greater love" because no other act of self-giving would carry the same abundance of love. Giving one's life for a friend embodies the force and dynamism of love in a way that could not be for a stranger or enemy.

Next we observe Jesus' unusual dictum that the disciples are his friends if they do whatever he tells them. A more disastrous basis for friendship can hardly be imagined! A healthy person would never agree to a friendship whose terms and conditions were that he always follow the wishes of the other. Obviously, however, this saying is not meant as a general prescription for the conduct of friendship! It must be remembered that the speaker is the Lord Jesus, and that the conditions are for friendship with him, not that of an ordinary man. What is the point of this verse? It is simply that friendship with Jesus is the highest realization of communion with him. As he is Lord, the condition of such communion is obedience to his commandments. To be his friend, one must open himself to his self-revelation and identify himself as fully as possible with the One who has offered himself. As a general principle, this is in keeping with the fundamental structure of true friendship: one opens himself to another and receives his self-offering. In the case of Jesus, this means embracing his teachings and keeping his commandments.

It is precisely the disciples' full reception of Jesus' self-revelation that enables him to recognize them as friends. In John's Last Supper discourse, Jesus finally discloses himself fully, completely, and without artifice to them. Their reaction to his monologue is telling: "See, now you are speaking plainly, and using no figure of speech!" (16:29). Now they are counted as his friends, for they have gladly received all that he revealed to them, confirming it by their faith in him: "Now we are sure that you know all things, and have no need that anyone should question you. By this we believe that you came forth from God" (16:30). For the first time, they have truly entered into communion with him. From being hearers, learners, and followers, they have become friends. They have entered into the mystery of his personhood, and he into theirs. Thus Jesus' final prayer for them (and all future believers) is a startling affirmation of the interpenetration of their spirits with his, and ultimately, the Father's: ". . . that they all may be one, as you, Father, are in me, and I in you; that they also may be one in us . . . that they may be one just as we are one . . . I in them and you in me; that they may be made perfect in one . . ." (17:21ab, 22b, 23a).

The communion of the disciples with Christ thus becomes a matter of spiritual union that partakes of God's eternity. The gospels go on to show that what begins in the world and in time will achieve its fullest possible realization in the eternal kingdom of God. In his account of the Last Supper, Mark's Gospel records these words as Jesus passes the cup to his disciples: "Assuredly, I say to you, I will no longer drink of the fruit of the vine until that day when I drink it anew in the kingdom of God" (14:25). Jesus here is not looking forward to the time in the kingdom when he will enjoy his next cup of wine. Rather, he is anticipating the resumption of the face-to-face feast at table with his friends in the fullness of the blessed kingdom. As the darkness of his impending passion approaches, it is as if he is saying to the disciples, "This is the last time we friends feast together in the world. But we shall feast anew and fully in the kingdom of God."

These strands of gospel teaching concerning Jesus' friendships thus leave us with the impression that the blessings of friendship carry intimations of the very life and nature of the heavenly kingdom. Certainly this is the case for friendship with Jesus. As we shall see more fully, it is also the case with all friendships that are grounded in him.

4 Notes

1. Kierkegaard is the best example. He discusses his rejection of friendship love at length in *You Shall Love Your Neighbor*, IIB (in Pakaluk, 235-247). "One must rather take pains to make very clear that the praise of erotic love and friendship belong to paganism . . . in order with the sure spirit of conviction to give to Christianity what belongs to Christianity, to love one's neighbor, of which love not a trace is found in paganism" (235).

2. It is interesting to observe the varying uses of the cognates of *philia* and *agape* in the gospel of John in the cases of Lazarus, Martha and Mary, the beloved disciple, and in his final dialogue with Peter (21:15-22). Although it would probably be going too far to say that the terms are interchangeable in John, they are certainly close synonyms. In some passages, it is difficult to say whether the variations are primarily stylistic or if a different emphasis is intended.

CHAPTER FIVE

Friendship in the Fathers

Although the biblical material on friendship is not voluminous, the key passages are of such clear significance that a distinct vision of friendship emerges from the relevant texts. In an Eastern Orthodox setting, it is important to consider how such biblical sources have been expressed in subsequent tradition. The witness of the Church Fathers is crucial in this regard. If numerous Fathers have carried forward the biblical witness on a particular theme, then we are not dealing with extrapolations from isolated biblical texts, but the tradition of the Church. To consider key patristic themes concerning friendship, we will follow the fine study of Carolinne White, *Christian Friendship in the Fourth Century*. As the fourth century is considered the epitome of the patristic era, a survey of its leading figures will provide the resources for elucidating the patristic witness on the subject.

Classical Influences on the Fathers

The fourth century Fathers were not only students of the Holy Scriptures, but men who lived and breathed the cultural atmosphere of the late antique period. As educated men of the era, they were deeply imbued with the influences of classical culture, and were inheritors of centuries of philosophical reflection on friendship by the ancient Greeks. The major Greek philosophers and schools devoted much attention to the topic, so much so that Aristotle's discussion remains the standard treatment of the subject to this day. Roman thinkers carried this interest forward. White summarizes the essential themes of the classical tradition as follows: "A fundamental belief in reciprocity as a *sine qua non* of friendship, a high degree of intimacy between two or at most a few persons which made it possible to think of a friend as a second self; the idea that a friend ought to possess some reason for being loved, which in the case of good men would be their virtue, and that friends should share material things and have interests in common" (55). There was nothing in the classical view that contradicted the biblical accounts, and as we shall see, the Fathers were concerned to integrate classical insights into a paradigm that was largely formed by distinctly Christian concerns.

Echoes of the classical perspective can be heard amid the distinctly Christian tones of Gregory the Theologian's writings. Speaking of his friend Basil the Great during the early years of their friendship, he writes, "We had all things in common, and a single soul, as it were, bound together in two distinct bodies. But above all it was God, of course, and a mutual desire for higher things, that drew us to each other. As a result, we reached such a pitch of confidence that we revealed the depths of our hearts, becoming ever more united in our yearning. There is no such solid bond of union as thinking the same thoughts" (63). Classical themes such as the intimacy of a friend as a "second self," the recognition of virtue in the other, the mutuality of interests, and the sharing of things in common are all represented in this passage. But his core conviction is that the origin of the friendship is in God and that its orientation is toward the pursuit of God. In all, we see substantial elements of the classical standpoint within an unmistakably Christian framework.

Gregory's comments provide an excellent starting point for consideration of specific themes relating to friendship as they are found in the Fathers. We will begin by addressing the problem of particular friendship in itself, then move to consider the qualities of friendship that are more natural and human, and finally proceed to those that are more distinctly Christian and divine.

Particular Friendships

A number of the Fathers clearly engaged in friendships that were particular and preferential. Yet does not giving special love and attention to one above others constitute a problem for Christians? This proved to be an issue especially within monastic communities, partially because preferential friendships were thought to be a potential temptation to sexual immorality. White explains that Basil held a more basic concern: "the law of love does not allow such friendships in a community, because they are seriously detrimental to the common harmony which is fostered by all the members feeling equal affection for the others; if someone has a particular affection for another monk it must mean that he is guilty of feeling less than perfect love for all the others" (82-3). Yet concerns that might be appropriate for those in monastic communities did not necessarily prevail for those outside. We know that Basil himself enjoyed special friendships with certain others, notably Gregory, particularly during his student days.

John Cassian has the wise Abba Joseph offer a different view in his Conferences. He uses the example of Jesus' special love for the Apostle John, which White summarizes as follows: " . . . this deep affection for one particular disciple did not imply that Jesus' love for the other disciples was lukewarm, but that he felt superabundant love for John because of John's chastity and purity. Far from condemning such special, partial feelings, Joseph regards them as more sublime, for to him they imply the perfection of virtue and great love" (180).

Gregory the Theologian justifies his special love for a

certain Nicoboulos by appealing to God's choice of one race as his own, and the fact that he was not deemed unjust for doing so (see 72). Most of the fourth century Fathers likely would have supported these arguments. Their writings indicate that they were aware of the special affinity one soul finds with a particular other. They did not see this as a hindrance, but rather as a stimulus to the pursuit of virtue. Their personal involvement in preferential friendships makes it clear that they found these friendships to be basically compatible with the Christian life, and even capable of enhancing it. Although they may have presented a potential problem in monastic communities, Fathers such as John Cassian saw that Lord's example endorsed the unique dynamics of close personal friendships.

However, certain Christian critics have been quick to point out that the classical approach to *philia* differs essentially from *agape*, the self-sacrificing Christian love of neighbor. Protestant writers in particular have been exercised over this problem to the point of rejecting *philia* as an unchristian affection. Their conviction is that the preferential character of *philia* is incompatible with *agape*, which is universal and offered equally to all.[1] White makes it clear, however, that this was not the approach of the Fathers. Although the outlook of each patristic writer was unique in its own regard, generally the Fathers accepted the validity of the classical view and the appropriateness of *philia*, but in fact went far beyond it themselves in the consideration of *agape*. They sought to ground friendship in the Divine Reality rather than in merely human phenomena, and endeavored to extend the mutual love of friendship outward into the Church and beyond even to enemies. As White points out, the Christian approach was not to abandon friendship as an inferior form of love, but to widen its scope considerably: "In fact the question of a conflict between the two seems not to have exercised the Fathers greatly because they were able to regard *philia* as a predominantly spiritual relationship . . ." (58).

Thus, in describing Augustine's teaching on friendship, Paul Wadell comments that, "Friendship is not inimical to the universal love of *agape*, but is the context in which *agape* is learned. It is its origins in the Spirit of love and its culmination in the kingdom of love that enables Christian friendship to be not an impediment, but a means to a more universal, inclusive, love" (101).

The virtues of the classical viewpoint found a sympathetic hearing among the Fathers, but they were not prepared to simply rest content with them as such. They took care to ground friendship in the distinctive perspectives of Christian faith. In this light, *philia* could be seen as instrumental to the development of *agape* rather than opposed to it.

Unity of Soul

One of the favorite patristic themes regarding friendship is that of a friend as a second self or as sharing the same soul. We have reflected on this phenomenon above and noted its presence in the Bible. It only remains for us to recognize the widespread patristic assent to the notion. Gregory indeed speaks of it eloquently; his sentiments are echoed by Chrysostom who knows and accepts the idea, and Ambrose who repeats it and adds that it is thus "very natural for a person to seek someone else to whose soul his own can cleave, thereby forming one entity" (121). It is clear that the Fathers, like their Greek philosophical forebears, recognized the mysterious communion that occurs between the souls of two persons who discover an inexplicable unity manifesting itself between them. As we shall see, Christian writers were not content to provide a merely human grounding for this phenomenon, but found its ultimate source in God.

Many Fathers recognized and revered the intimacy and trust that support the unity of soul between friends as great treasures. Ambrose wrote: "Preserve, my sons, that friendship which you have begun with your brother; for nothing in the world is more beautiful than that. It is indeed a comfort in this life to have someone to whom you can open your heart, with whom you can share confidences and to whom you can entrust the secrets of your heart. It is a comfort to have someone trustworthy beside you who will share your happiness, sympathize with your troubles, and encourage you in persecution" (118). We noted above Gregory's testimony to Basil that "we reached such a pitch of confidence that we revealed the depths of our hearts, becoming ever more united in our yearning. There is no such solid bond of union as thinking the same thoughts."

Such testimony to the unity of thought and sentiment between friends emphasizes the value of both intimacy and trust. In this vein, both Augustine and Jerome refer to Cicero's idea that a friend is a person with whom one can discuss everything as with oneself (see 139, 193). Augustine writes to a certain Profuturus, "You know all this, but since you are a second self to me, how could I wish to say anything to you apart from what I say to myself?" (194). These Fathers saw that the intimate union between true friends runs so deep that talking with one's friend is as comfortable as thinking to oneself.

Cicero had laid great stress on the fact that friends inevitably share a consensus of opinion on a wide range of matters. He described friendship as "a relationship based on agreement about all human and divine matters, together with good will and affection," and added "when the character of friends is blameless then there should be between them complete harmony of opinions in everything without exception" (32, 33). What seems like a possibly unrealistic standard is reflected in the Fathers as an ideal; they certainly emphasized the value of unanimity of view, but were perhaps less rigorous in applying it to every facet of life. Augustine had a positive evaluation of how occasions of disagreement could function within healthy relationships: "We could talk and laugh together and exchange small acts of kindness. Together we could read delightful books and we could be serious and joke together. Sometimes we would disagree but without any ill-feeling, just as a man differs with himself and even these rare instances of disagreement added spice to our usual agreement. We could all teach each other something and learn from one another" (212).

Of course, the unity of thought and sentiment between friends presupposes that they freely open their hearts and fully reveal themselves to each other. Ambrose saw the connection we have made above with the example of Jesus: "If he is a true friend he will hide nothing; he will reveal his soul completely just as our Lord Jesus revealed the mysteries of his Father"(122). The free and honest self-revelation inherent in true friendship produces great delight in the friends, as Chrysostom recognized: "The pleasure of friendship excels all others, even if you compare it with the sweetness of honey, for that satiates, but a friend never does"(92). Gregory the Theologian is blunt and to the point: "If anyone were to ask me, 'What is the best thing in life?,' I would answer, 'Friends' " (70).

Unity and Separation

When friendship is esteemed so highly, it is natural that periods of separation would bring about intense longing for the company of one's friend. Augustine writes of his friends, "When we were apart we missed our friends sorely but welcomed each other joyfully on our return" (212). Chrysostom wrote his dearest friend Olympias to the effect that that separation from a loving soul is no small trial and one that requires a "philosophical" mind. He held that it is not enough for those who love one another to be spiritually united, they also need one another's physical presence, for otherwise a large part of their joy is removed (see 97). Some consolation could be had, however, in the belief that friends could be present to one another in their minds so that they could be close to one another in their thoughts when they could not be together physically, as Augustine maintained (see 209). Synesius of Cyrene[2] expressed this idea eloquently in a letter to his friend Olympius, where he stated, "Even when you are absent you are always present to me in my thoughts, for even if I really wanted to, I could not forget the sweetness of your soul and your honest disposition. Nothing could be more precious to me than my memory of you, nothing except the prospect of embracing you again" (103).

Where physical togetherness was impossible, letters helped bridge the gap. The value of letters to maintaining friendships was obvious both to classical authors as well as the Christian Fathers. It was widely recognized that letters had the ability to make a friend present that was otherwise absent. The correspondence of Synesius, a man who intensely valued his friendships, makes abundant reference to this concept (see 107). Likewise, John Chrysostom's letters to Olympias passionately plead for letters of response from her, in the belief that this was the only way they could ward off the pain of separation and experience the intimacy that existed between their souls.

The Breakdown of Friendships

Since these Fathers envisioned genuine friendship as characterized by deep intimacy, trust, and unity, the breakdown of friendships posed a thorny problem. Some Fathers, such as John Chrysostom, held that true friendships could never be dissolved because the spiritual bond between friends is more powerful than any threat to it (see 93). Jerome, in one of his early letters, wrote, "Friendship that can cease cannot be genuine"(129). Yet some years later Jerome became embroiled in a bitter controversy with his (former) friend Rufinus, whom he castigated in the sharpest terms (see 132). Gregory, who had spoken so glowingly of his friendship with Basil, later was gravely disappointed in his friend and wrote bitterly of his disillusionment with him (see 66-68). These examples are telling because such men all remained devoted Christians throughout their lives, and yet they were unable to maintain bonds of friendship that had once enraptured them.

John Cassian gives a thorough analysis of this problem in the sixteenth chapter of his *Conferences*. There the Abba Joseph discourses at length about friendship, and pays special attention to the problem of why friendships break down. He points out that many friendships lack a strong spiritual foundation, and thus are subject to decline when both parties no longer share common worldly interests and desires. His opinion is that shared virtue is the only sound basis for friendship, and that both friends must maintain equal fervor for their purpose, or the friendship will dissolve. Writing from within a monastic context, he sees ascetical purification as a necessary component to lasting friendship, because that will obviate the baneful influences of self-will and egotism (see 177). A person must be cleansed of the harmful effects of the passions if he is to be a true friend. Having been thus purified, he is capable of maintaining friendships in a healthy manner. Such friendships are not threatened with dissolution but partake of eternity.

As attractive as this theory may sound, it does not account for the fact that the above-mentioned Fathers experienced painful ruptures in friendships in spite of being both dedicated Christians and accomplished in the ascetical life. It may be simpler to understand this problem in light of the basic rule that friends generally share a nearly complete harmony of opinions. This is the condition for the development of the sense of unity between them. As we have noted, incidental disagreements should not threaten a good friendship. But where there is a difference of opinions on matters of critical importance, friendships can and do unravel. An essential support to the unity between friends collapses and the damage is often too substantial for the relationship to survive. At some level, the covenant between them has been breached. What is left intact cannot sustain the friendship.

However, while a number of the Fathers personally experienced the painful rupture of close friendships, mainstream patristic thought continued to uphold permanence as the ideal for genuine friendship. They did not hesitate to ascribe the immutability of true friendships to the fact that they are grounded in God. We thus turn our attention to the role of the Divine in the formation and maintenance of friendships.

God: The Source of Friendship

Gregory's belief that God draws friends together is characteristic of many Fathers. Their sense is that the occurrence of friendship is a manifestation of the unfolding of divine destiny. It is also the work of the Holy Spirit drawing two souls into profound unity. Chrysostom is sure that godly friendships have a heavenly origin (see 93). Paulinus of Nola connected the conviction that God creates friendships with the idea that he has predestined certain men to be friends from the beginning of time (see 155). Because of this, he held that these friendships are perfect from the very beginning: "Please do not measure our friendship in terms of time. For ours is not that worldly kind of friendship . . . but the spiritual friendship sprung from the fatherhood of God and joined through the hidden kinship of the spirit . . . since it arises from Christ, it overflows at the very start" (155). In another letter, he avers, "We have become known to each other not by human friendship but by divine grace and it is by inner depths of Christ's love that we are joined. Therefore between our hearts there must inevitably abide that perennial harmony which was joined at Christ's instigation, for what force or forgetfulness can separate what God has joined together?" (155).

White sums up the thought of Synesius: " . . . God not only watches over friendships, he also creates them . . . and keeps friends united by being present to them even during periods of separation" (106). Synesius himself recognizes that there are merely earthly friendships, but asserts there are others over which Divinity presides, and asserts that he fuses those who love one another so that from being two they become one (see 106). Augustine held that love and friendship are given by the grace of God, rather than being a merely human phenomenon, writing that "There can be no true friendship unless God cements the bond between two people by means of the love poured forth in our hearts by the Holy Spirit which he has granted to us" (196). These deep convictions hearken back to the oath between Jonathan and David: "The Lord be between you and me forever." They are based on the sense that the mystery of communion between friends participates in a dimension greater than itself, and is the subject of a transcendental assimilation. In other words, God draws the friends together in the communion of his own Spirit. Divine grace is the common medium shared by pious friends and the ontological bridge between their souls.

Unity in the Body of Christ

This insight is solidified by the grounding of friendships in the Church as the body of Christ. According to Basil the Great, the fact that Christians are members of the body of Christ and united by spiritual love means that there should be a deep unity between them (see 75). White holds that Basil's desire was "to restore the Church to a kind of friendship where all the members of Christ's body are united as close friends dedicated to serving God according to the true faith" (77). A prevalent patristic view was thus to see the unity of Christ's body as the living bond that joins the souls of friends together.

White sums up the approach of Paulinus of Nola ". . . as soon
as two committed Christians realize they are bound together in
friendship, a great leap in spiritual progress can be regarded as
being made, for from that moment they can feel Christ between
them, and loving each other they prove that they are truly disciples of the one who laid down his life for his friends" (156).
"Christ between us" is the essential element of their unity.

This unity is so real for Paulinus that "a more practical
consequence of friends being members of one spiritual body
was apparently that they would share one another's feelings and
illnesses" (157). The sense of a palpable unity between friends
in the one body of Christ was upheld by Basil, who stressed
"the profound interdependence of its members who need one
another and are so closely involved with one another that they
will experience deep sympathy for one another's joys and sorrows" (76). This sympathy, however, is more that just "feeling
for" another; rather, it is entering the experience of the other.
The relationship between John Chrysostom and Olympias demonstrates this poignantly. Chrysostom's love for her was such
that her feelings became his, even when he was quite far away
from her (see 96).

Like other Fathers, Augustine grounds the unity between
Christian friends in the body of Christ. He asks, "Is not the
main aim of friends to become one?" and then adds, "and the
more united they are, the closer friends they become" (208).
For him, as for Basil, this closeness is best realized in community life. Regardless of its social context, however, the closeness of friends is the source of a shared emotional life that
when fully spiritually intense, is a realization of the life of the
glorified Christ himself. Marie McNamara thus writes that
"Augustine's ideal of perfect unity is perfect friendship among
men who are joined through love inseparably to Christ, so that
all together form the 'one Christ loving himself'" (in Wadell,
103).

Unity and the Trinity

Ultimately, the unity of friends in the one body of Christ leads certain Fathers to see friendship as an image of the unity of the Holy Trinity. Ambrose uses human friendship to aid in the understanding of the Trinity, pointing out that like true friends, there is no difference in the divine persons in substance or will (see 127). Augustine sees friendship as having its origin in the "friendship" that God is, Trinitarian love (see Wadell, 99).

We thus turn our attention to the ultimate source and ground of the phenomenon of human friendship, the Orthodox Christian conviction that God himself is a communion of persons in love and freedom.

5 Notes

1. Anders Nygren carries forward Kierkegaard's dialectic between biblical and pagan forms of love especially with regard to *eros*. Although he is not concerned as much with *philia* per se, his critique follows the same lines as Kierkegaard's in exalting *agape* as the only truly Christian form of love. Their distinctly evangelical position strictly opposes what is natural and human to what is divine.

2. Synesius of Cyrene is not numbered among the Fathers of the Church. An interesting figure, he was an fourth-century Christian bishop who, according to White, was more a thoroughgoing Neoplatonist than a believing Christian (see 98-100).

CHAPTER SIX

A Theology of Friendship

Understanding Christian friendship as an experience of communion in love has led us to consider the elements that render the sense of shared selfhood possible. Our review of patristic views on friendship saw them grounded in the body of Christ and ultimately revealed the Holy Trinity as the supreme prototype of such communion. We now turn our attention to bringing these insights together and sketching out a theology of friendship, reflecting on how the human experience of friendship relates to the being of God.[1]

There are several fundamental themes that will guide our inquiry: human existence as the realization of personal freedom in love, the Holy Trinity as the essential ground of relational personhood, and the communion of human persons in the Person of the glorified Christ. At this level of investigation, the theology of John Zizioulas in his *Being as Communion* will be our guide.

Personhood, Freedom, and Love

Zizioulas, like a number of modern Orthodox theologians, makes a distinction between the biological existence of man and personhood realized in freedom through love. Though he affirms the role of love as ecstatic self-giving in the act of procreation, Zizioulas points out that the biological nature of reproduction is rooted in natural necessity. Though one's parents may indeed have expressed sexual love freely, the sexual origination of human existence itself is a non-negotiable given. The biological constitution of one's existence is thus a fact of the human condition and not an achievement of personal existence in freedom.[2] To illustrate this, Zizioulas quotes one of Dostoevsky's characters questioning, "And who consulted me when I was brought into the world?" (50). One's existence is first of all a brute biological fact. This Zizioulas calls the "ontological necessity" of human existence. It is nothing less than human *createdness*, a sheer givenness that is not yet freedom.

Zizioulas sees individualism as the natural consequence of man's bodily and biological reality. Every human being is an individual human unit with built-in biological needs related to survival. In this respect, his own identity is defined over against others, with whom he must compete for the means necessary to maintain bodily existence. Ultimately, one's biological nature is perpetuated by the very means one came to exist in the first place, "through the creation of bodies, that is, of hypostatic unities which affirm their identity as separation from other unities or 'hypostases'" (51). The continuation of individual existence through ingestion, digestion, elimination, and procreation is the motivating drive in every human being, and is a biological phenomenon foreign to freedom. It comes to full fruition in the identification of the self as the separate existence of an ego wearing the "mask" of the body and preoccupied with carrying on its own life. Unfortunately, it is circumscribed by the inescapable demise of individual biological life in death, which Zizioulas sees as the inevitable final destiny of biological individualism.

In contrast to the deterministic nature of the human biological constitution, Zizioulas sets forth the reality of man in the Church, "the hypostasis of ecclesial existence" (see 53ff.). In the ecclesial context, man is realized solely through freedom in love. Zizioulas' demonstration of this is complex and difficult to summarize. Basically, he shows that the realization of true human personhood can only take place when humanity is no longer grounded in the necessity of createdness. This transformation is achieved when Jesus Christ, the *uncreated* Person of the Eternal Son of God, unites himself to human nature. Christ manifests the perfect human realization of freedom and love, and in him, each human existence may be reconfigured anew in the same orientation. Zizioulas writes, "Thanks to Christ, man can henceforth himself 'subsist,' can affirm his existence as personal, not on the basis of the immutable laws of his nature, but on the basis of a relationship with God which is identified with what Christ in freedom and love possesses as Son of God with the Father" (56). He then points out that in the Church, new relationships are formed which parallel those of the biological family, but in a manner free from the dictates of biology, being formed only by love in freedom. Accordingly, "This means that henceforth (the ecclesial person) can love not because the laws of biology oblige him to do so – something which inevitably colors the love of one's own relations – but *unconstrained* by the natural laws" (57). Relationships in the Church are based purely in the free identification of the self with Christ and with others in him.

Friendship and Freedom

The implications of this reasoning for the subject of friendship, especially Christian friendship, are readily apparent. For what is friendship, but precisely an actualization of love born purely in freedom? Friends are those whose affinity for each other has no biological connection. Their relationship may have its origins in situations that are purely accidental (workplace, school, etc.), but the peculiar relation of friendship depends precisely on the free will of persons to associate with each other in this unique way.

If anything is clear about friendships, it is that forces of necessity do not create them. It may be argued that it is necessary to have friends but particular friendships are always a manifestation of freedom. We have seen above that close friends often sense an element of "destiny," "fate," or inevitability about their relationship. However, this is not an assertion of a deterministic necessity overruling the freedom of the individual friends, but an affirmation of the transcendent qualities of the bond between them. It is a way of expressing the perception that the friendship is a greater reality than the mere coupling of the individuals. In actuality, freedom is an irreducible core element of all friendships.

Friends may indeed experience an inner drive to be with each other that almost feels like a compulsion, especially as an intense friendship begins to form. Except in cases where neurotic need is behind this desire, however, it remains very much a matter of will. Certainly, the sudden discovery of a broad compatibility and deep communion with another is a very powerful force that seems to impel people to be together. But this is because they so very much *want* to be together that they *will* to be together.

Friends freely *decide* to associate with each other, spend time together, keep up their conversation, engage in mutual activities, trust each other, show their love to one another, stay in contact when apart, and maintain their relationship after moving away from each other. Or they may decide to allow their friendship to fizzle out for any number of reasons. In any case, by their very nature, friendships are manifestations of love that are entirely rooted in freedom. Andrew Sullivan's commentary is apt: "[Friends] enter into friendship as an act of radical choice. Friendship, in this sense, is the performance art of freedom" (212).

There is thus never the same sense of obligation about friendships that characterizes family relationships. The difference is that family relationships are grounded in the biological necessity of the perpetuation of the species, and thus are inescapably bound up with unconscious compulsion. Friendship does not have this quality. Commenting on Montaigne, Sullivan sums it up well: "The essential fact about family is that it is unchosen, and because it is unchosen, it does not belong in the same category of moral freedom and excellence as friendship" (226). Of course, this is not to say that *philia* is not present in family relationships. It certainly can be, and in the case of marriage, it is essential. Friendship, however, is more purely an exercise of freedom.

The Achievement of Personhood

In the categories of Zizioulas, friendship can be seen as a pathway toward the actualization of true human *personhood*. For him, personhood is bound up with the concreteness, uniqueness, and unrepeatability of each human being. However, one's unique identity in the world is originally a way of defining oneself *over against* others: "I am I; you are you." How can the tendency of personhood toward division (and for Zizioulas, ultimately, death) be overcome? Only by the self-transcendence of love. Love, freely given, manifests the essential relatedness of a person to others. Thus the individual who cannot love fails to develop true personhood, or is in the process of divesting himself of it. On the contrary, the one who loves fully becomes his own identity through communion with others. "I know who I am only I because I have encountered you as you and valued you as you." The element of valuation is critical. If I do not value you, I have not really taken you into account, and thus I remain locked into the limitations of my own self. This valuation, this existence of the self "toward and for the other," is the essential precondition for love.

77

The achievement of human personhood therefore is unthinkable apart from the drive for communion.[3] It is undeniable that relatedness is a fact of human existence from the moment of our conception. We are conceived in the fire of passionate relations between two people. We develop in the nurturing womb of our mother. We experience our relatedness first at her breast, and then with our father and siblings, relatives and neighbors. We find out soon enough that our existence has occurred in the nexus of particular communities, and then discover the place of those communities in the larger realm of the human race in the world. We venture into friendships, integrate into all kinds of associations, find lovers, marry, and beget children. Even the most distinctly biological aspects of our generation and socialization do not and cannot occur apart from personal relationships. When one becomes fully conscious, one recognizes the dimension of communion that is possible, may actually underlie, and is often manifest in such relationships. The highest and most fulfilling are those in which a genuine experience of communion between persons takes place in utter freedom: friendships and marriage. The essential relatedness of all human life thus places us in a position where we seek to achieve our ultimate fulfillment in true communion with others, unless our development has been stymied by a dysfunctional socialization. Living the event of such communion, we can be truly said to be "persons."

John MacMurray has summed up these fundamental insights in a statement that echoes the insights of John Zizioulas and has an almost "creedal" ring to it: "Thus human experience is, in principle, shared experience; human life, even in its most individual elements, is a common life; and human behavior carries always, in its inherent structure, a reference to the personal Other. All this may be summed up by saying that the unit of personal existence is not the individual, but two persons in personal relation; and that we are persons not by individual right, but in virtue of our relation to one another. The personal is constituted by personal relatedness. The unit of the person is not the 'I', but the 'You and I'" (61).

The Holy Trinity: Prototype of Personhood in Relation

Zizioulas thus asserts "The significance of the person rests in the fact that he represents two things simultaneously which are at first sight in contradiction: particularity and communion. Being a person is fundamentally different from being an individual or a 'personality' for a person cannot be imagined in himself but only within his relationships" (105). This conviction that personhood is grounded in relationship ultimately is rooted in patristic teaching concerning the Holy Trinity. In their adoption and recasting of the Greek term "hypostasis" with regard to the persons of the Holy Trinity, the Fathers effectively demonstrated, according to Zizioulas, that to be and to be in relation are identical (see 88).

In the Orthodox vision, God as Holy Trinity is not a being, essence, or substance in which the persons subsist as subsequent "relations." Rather, God is known as the unoriginate Father who eternally begets his only-begotten Son and emits his life-giving Spirit in the fullness of uncreated Deity. Since the generation of the Son and the procession of the Spirit are eternal, the Father is eternally "father;" that is, God himself is an eternal relationship. The being of God is specifically the communion of persons. His essence is not prior to an act of communion but is precisely the act of communion. Personally distinct from the Father, the Son and Spirit are of "one essence" with Him in the reality of communion.

Commenting on Athanasius, Zizioulas concludes "*communion belongs not to the level of will and action, but to that of substance*" (86, italics his). He then laments theological and philosophical developments in which a rupture has taken place between being and communion, resulting in the idea that individuality is the fundamental characteristic of being. In this view, "... the world ultimately consists as a fragmentary existence, in which beings are particular *before* they can relate to each other: first you *are* and then you relate" (103, italics his).

We have seen how human existence, like the being of God, is relational at the very root.[4] Given the creation of humanity in the image and likeness of God, this is not a surprise. It remains for us to explore the particular ways in which friendship reflects the life of the God who is the primordial reality of communion.

Friendship and the Communion of Persons

It is a basic Christian dogma that the Father, Son, and Holy Spirit are fully personal in every respect in the communion of the one divine nature. The experience of human friendship is that in which full persons achieve genuine communion in the one human nature. Each one is a distinct and particular person in his own right, and yet friends find their common humanity to be the source of essential unity between them. This unity of nature underlying the particular relationship is the dimension that undergirds the experience of being "one soul."

Since all human beings share the one human nature, what is it about a friendship that generates and heightens the experience of essential oneness? What is it about a particular relationship among others that reveals this fundamental unity? Is it not the basic agreement of attitude, perception, experience, and will that exists among friends?

Such vital concord itself mirrors the life of the Trinity. The unity of the divine persons is grounded in the divine essence in which the Son and Spirit subsist because of their origin in the Father. It is manifest in the absolute harmony and agreement in the Deity with regard to every manifestation of the divine will. Every act of God originates in the Father, is constituted in the Son and accomplished in the Holy Spirit as one operation. One mind and one will exist among the three divine hypostases.

As we have seen, the Fathers of the Church emphasize oneness of mind and agreement of will as essential characteristics of true friendship. When we consider the experience of unity of nature, oneness of mind, and agreement of will among friends, the spiritual aspects of the relationship become apparent. Friendship reveals the essential truth of being human in the image and likeness of God. It is an icon of the life of the Holy Trinity and means of participation in the very nature of Ultimate Reality, which is nothing less than Being as Communion.

Communion in the New Adam

We may ask what the anthropological ground of this phenomenon is, what makes it possible. This question immediately leads us to considerations of Christology and ecclesiology. Ultimately, to understand friendship theologically, we must understand critical aspects of the nature of Adam, the nature of Jesus Christ, and the nature of the Church.

Leaving aside the question of how literally one ought to read Genesis, it is clear in the light of Zizioulas' theology that Adam is a hypostasis but not an individual. In himself, as originally created, Adam is *humanity*; he encompasses all humanity in his body. Thus Eve is taken from his body and Adam remarks, "This is bone of my bone and flesh of my flesh." Since they are originally one body, the unitive drive between man and woman exists to reclaim their original oneness of flesh: "*Therefore* shall a man leave father and mother and cleave unto his wife, and the two shall be *one flesh*." Every subsequent human individual comes from that original oneness. Thus, to repeat, originally all humanity and every possible human person exist in the one humanity of Adam. It can be accurately stated that he is a corporate person. But Adam falls and is no longer able to be the unifying hypostasis of humanity. Mankind fragments into individuals whose existence is opposed to each other: in the first generation after Adam, Cain murders Abel.

Because of the failure of Adam and the resulting fragmentation of mankind into individuality, the eternal Son of God takes on and recreates human nature in all its fullness as the second Adam. His mission is to reintegrate humanity once again into one hypostasis, his own deified humanity.

Because of this, the New Testament speaks in very realistic terms about the incorporation of believers into the body of Christ. The physical members of a Christian's body are extensions of Christ's existence: "Shall I take the members of Christ and unite them to a prostitute?" (I Cor. 6:15) Paul asks. He is vitally aware that even the physical body of a Christian has been integrated into the glorified hypostasis of Christ. The epistle to the Ephesians thus makes it clear that the glorified existence of Christ now includes the existence of all who have been incorporated into him through baptism. The fullness of Christ's glorified life includes the Church, "the fullness of him who fills all in all" (Eph. 1:23). Christ is the new Adam whose hypostasis integrates the entirety of the new humanity, the Church. It is on this basis that Zizioulas vigorously rejects the notion that Christ is an individual. He asserts that it is impossible to speak of the resurrected Christ other than in terms of communion (see 113-114n.). Since his glorification, one cannot consider the head apart from the body, which is the Church, the fullness of the new humanity united to him by faith.

In the unity of the one body of Christ, believers are all

integrated into one living organism. They share one common life. One blood courses through the veins of the one body and nourishes them all. One Spirit indwells the body and each of its members. The Apostle Paul vividly portrays the life of the body as a vital unity: "For as the body is one and has many members, but all the members of that one body, being many, are one body, *so also is Christ.* For by one Spirit we were all baptized into one body" (I Cor. 12:12-3). This unity is so real that "if one member suffers, all the members suffer with it; or if one member is honored, all the members rejoice with it – now you are the body of Christ and members individually" (26-7).

Spiritual Unity in Friendship

At this point we can understand the basis for the deep experiences of unity among friends in Christ. Even apart from Christ, profound empathy among friends can be observed. Such friends indeed share the one human nature created in the image of God, though fallen in Adam. Additionally, they may share a wide variety of historical experiences, beliefs, convictions, perceptions, and other potential natural sources of unity. It is altogether likely that non-Christian friends are able to participate directly in each other's feelings and ideas.

In the body of Christ, however, a new dimension of human unity is achieved. Christian friends share a common way of life, have a common core identity, and participate in a common dimension of Spirit in the unity of Christ's body. Thus they have a heightened potential for direct soul-to-soul contact and knowledge, such as that experienced by John Chrysostom and Olympias. The empathic phenomena that passed between them were grounded in their unity in Christ. Their lives were taken up and integrated into the glorified hypostasis of the new Adam, and thus the actuality of oneness in Christ was beneath their unusual experience of oneness.

A deep mystic knowledge of and identification with the life of others has been characteristic of many saints. St. Silouan of Athos is a good example. Speaking of the spiritual vision of a such a true Orthodox ascetic, his biographer, Archimandrite Sophrony, writes, "He thus finds his *deep* heart – reaches the profound spiritual, metaphysical core of his being; and looking into it he sees that the existence of mankind is not something alien and extraneous to him but is inextricably bound up with his own existence. 'Our brother is our life' the Staretz (Silouan) often said. Through Christ's love, all men are made an inseparable part of our own individual, eternal existence. The Staretz began to understand the commandment, Love thy neighbor as thyself, as something more than an ethical imperative. In the word *as* he saw an indication, not of a required degree of love but of an *ontological community of being* . . . as a kind of revelation of what is happening in the world at large. Every form of pain and suffering . . . is lived not only within the self, 'selfishly,' but is transferred in spirit to other people . . . In this fashion, those who practice obedience develop Christian compassion for the torment of all humanity, and their prayers take on a cosmic dimension embracing the whole Adam – in other words, their prayer becomes *hypostatic*, after the manner of Christ's prayer in Gethsemane. This sort of prayer makes man aware of his unity with all mankind, and to love his neighbor – his fellow man – becomes a natural impulse" (31, 85-86 italics his). For the deified saint, the experience of empathy embraces all humanity. His soul touches and knows that of countless others. This is the source of the well-known "clairvoyance" characteristic of many Orthodox saints.

If such is true of saints, perhaps those of lesser spiritual attainment may experience a similar empathy with those to whom they are closest in Christ: their friends. It would seem that the love of friends on occasion may transcend the boundaries of the ordinary and pass into spiritual dimensions of intimacy that for most people are little known and even less easily explained. One can only recognize such experiences for what they are and affirm their fundamental source as the unity of the one human hypostasis of the new Adam.

Philosopher Max Picard thus concludes: "In the world of Faith, friendship lies in bringing out clearly in the relation between two human beings that which in itself is not evident, the solidarity (*Verbundenheit*) of all men. Friendship between two human beings is a testimony to the universal solidarity and as such a testimony it endures" (62). He adds, "Two friends, for example, need not in their friendship begin at the beginning. They can live together in friendship at once, as though their intimacy had been a long one: for in the world of Faith they can also share in the friendship existing over and above their personal friendship" (67).

The ultimate horizon of human friendship is the eternal divine relationship of the Holy Trinity. Through their incorporation into the God-man Jesus Christ, Christian friends are granted participation in that divine communion. Commenting on Augustine, Paul Wadell avers that "The friendship that God is, this Trinitarian love, is the friendship from which human friendships begin, the love to which they must conform, and the community in which they are perfected" (99). We turn our attention now to how indeed friendships in the body of Christ find their perfection in the unity of the Father and communion of the Holy Spirit.

6 Notes

1. Paul Florensky sets forth the challenge to explore the revelatory power of friendship. Speaking of transfigured, spiritualized existence as the manifestation of the heavenly realm in the earthly, he writes, "This revelation occurs in the personal, sincere love of two, in friendship, when to the loving one is given – in a preliminary way, without ascesis – the power to overcome his self-identity, to remove the boundaries of his I, to transcend himself, and to acquire his own I in the I of another, a Friend. Friendship, as the mysterious birth of *Thou*, is the environment in which the revelation of the Truth begins" (283, italics his).

2. John MacMurray has clearly demonstrated, however, that the personal dimension is never absent from the most nascent human existence. Speaking of an infant, he writes, "He is born into a love-relationship which is inherently personal. Not merely his personal development, but his very survival depends upon the maintaining of this relation; he depends on it for his existence, that is to say, upon intelligent understanding, upon rational foresight. He cannot think for himself, yet he cannot do without thinking; someone else must think for him . . . Now if we attend to these everyday facts without any theoretical prejudice, it is obvious that the relation of mother and child is quite inadequately expressed in biological terms . . ." (48-49). MacMurray's observations qualify Zizioulas' speculation about a purely biological individualism: there is no phase of human life that is purely biological, non-personal and non-relational. At most Zizioulas presents stylizations of human life that are

emphatically drawn for the sake of contrast.

3. MacMurray makes the *personal* nature of the mother-child relationship a fundamental principle of his relational approach to human existence. "The mother not only does what is needful for the child: she fondles him, caresses him, rocks him in her arms, and croons to him; and the baby responds with expressions of delight in his mother's care which have no biological significance. These gestures symbolize a mutual delight in the relation which unites them in a common life: they are expressions of affection through which each communicates to the other their delight in the relationship . . ." (63).

4. Florensky sees this truth, and like Zizioulas, immediately recognizes its full realization in ecclesial life: "The person can be absolutely valuable only in absolutely valuable communion, although one cannot say that the person is prior to communion or that communion is prior to the person. The primordial person and primordial communion, which rationally are seen as excluding each other, are given as a fact in Church life. They are given together and at the same time" (302).

CHAPTER SEVEN

Friendship in Christian Life

A vision of friendship that sees its source and ground in the eternal communion of the Holy Trinity ought to bear potential for spiritual fruitfulness. Accordingly, the inherent spiritual qualities of Christian friendship should result in tangible benefits in the Christian life. Understanding friendship from an Orthodox Christian perspective thus is not a matter of merely elaborating an adequate theory. It entails showing its practical implications for the salvation and restoration of the human person. In his *Friendship and the Moral Life*, Paul Wadell has elegantly portrayed the rich and dynamic role that friendships play in the development of a godly life. His description of the *praxis* of friendship beautifully fleshes out the *theoria* of friendship that we have sketched out above.

Friendship and Moral Development

Wadell describes how his reading of Aristotle articulated for him "something of which I was always convinced, that friendships are not only enjoyable, but highly morally formative . . ." He goes on to explain how this insight developed, that "The moral life is the seeking of and growing in the good in the company of friends who also want to be good. Friendship is the crucible of the moral life, the relationship in which we come to embody the good by sharing it with friends who also delight in the good" (xiii).

This notion, which may seem obvious upon reflection, may appear stunningly novel at first. "We live in a culture of individualism which tends to view the moral life as being concerned with inner subjective dispostitions and personal dilemmas." Most modern ethical discussion tends to view the moral agent as an autonomous self struggling with problems raised by the existence of others. In this context, ethics often degenerates into a process of ascertaining guidelines for individuals to make informed and proper decisions. A solitary self faced with difficult choices almost always occupies the stage of modern ethical reflection.

In keeping with the fundamental theological themes we have outlined above, however, Wadell approaches the moral life and godliness from the viewpoint of a self-in-relation. This approach demands that we recognize that our native traditions have inculcated in us a particular sense of godliness and moral life. The role of specific exemplars and instructors in these traditions is especially important to our early moral formation. As we mature and grow, companions who embrace the journey toward the good join us and sometimes replace early exemplars and instructors. It is precisely in the context of such relationships that the good is usually pursued and discovered. Few indeed are the hermits and anchorites who have found perfection in the isolation of their desert caves. Much more numerous are those who have lived out blessedness in community with others.

After a moving reminiscence of his days in seminary, Wadell makes a profound summary of the role of friends in the formation of moral character: "The moral life is often such retrospective activity because sooner or later we try to understand what has made us who we are. This leads us to certain people. We remember them, we cherish them, we are grateful to them because we realize we could not have been ourselves without them. We call these people friends . . . When we think of the moral life, it is not surprising we think of them. They taught us the good. They formed us. Through their love they chiseled in us qualities we could not have reached alone. When we think of the moral life, we do not remember only the decisions we sometimes had to make, even the problems that may have beset us, we also remember our friends and the life that was shared between us. *There seemed to be nothing better than to be with them, that somehow being with them was being oursel* (sic), *that somehow who we were was exactly the friendships that meant so much to us"* (7, italics mine). Clearly, then, friends help constitute not only our moral character, but our larger identity as well. This is inherent in the very nature of the selves-in-relation that we are.

How in fact do our friends form us morally? Without attempting to be exhaustive, we may recognize that the Christian life is essentially the process of acquiring and growing in virtue, that is, habits of godliness. The nature of any virtue is the achievement of likeness to God in some particular respect. The most basic prerequisite for a morally formative friendship is therefore mutual commitment to virtue. Wadell thus elaborates, "Virtues require stable, enduring relationships. But they also require good relationships. Virtues are habits we develop by practice, but we must learn what it means to practice a particular virtue and have the opportunity to grow in it through relationships with others who share our hunger for the good. Growth in virtue is not accidental; it takes place through the ongoing relationships we have with people who are one with us in what we consider important, one with us in what we most deeply desire. These people are our best and closest friends, and because what we desire matters to them as well, it is with and through them that our moral development primarily occurs" (xiv).

The Unity of Friends and the Kingdom of God

Friendships make moral life possible because they represent a successful passage through the original ethical situation – the encounter with the other – to a deep identification of the self with another. They highlight the reality that humanity is a community of being. The means through this passageway is the development of a habitual disposition of kindness toward another, another who does not have any prior natural claim on oneself, such as family relationship. Thus the affinity and affection between friends represents the achievement of the ideal of human relations, a bond rooted in a deep care for another and expressed in a willingness to sacrifice one's own well-being for one's friend. "Greater love has no man than this, that a man lay down his life for his friends" (John 15:13).

Yet Christian critics over the centuries, as we have seen, have impugned friendship because of its exclusive character. Even Zizioulas, who does not discuss friendship, describes the love typical of the ecclesial person as transcending "every exclusiveness of a biological or social kind" (60). From the frequency with which the issue is raised, it would seem that the necessarily preferential and exclusive nature of friendship raises a thorny theological problem. Yet ultimately, Zizioulas concludes that " . . . love, which, while it can concentrate on one person as the expression of the whole nature, sees in this person the hypostasis through which all men and all things are loved . . ." (63). The love of all can be found in the love of one person. In particular, with regard to friendship, the experience of the unity of human nature in the love of another person is very much the love of all expressed in the love for a friend.

Wadell thus answers those who feel that friendship ("loving those who love you") is an inferior form of love as follows: "As Christians grow in agape they do not leave their friendships behind, for the Kingdom is ultimately what their friendships become. The center of their friendships is always Christ, that is why the Kingdom represents not a different love, but an extension of the community formed by that love. This is why we can say the perfect bonding of all men and women to one another in Christ signifies not a love other than friendship, but the unity for which Christian friendship always strove" (103). Thus Christians are not called to leave aside friendships to pursue the more noble love that is *agape*, rather they are to extend the realm of their friendship love as far as possible into the wider human community.

The Blessings of Spiritual Companionship

The ways in which Christian friends manifest their soulunity are pathways that link the kingdom of heaven to this earth. A famous passage from Ecclesiastes reminds us that "Two are better than one, because they have a good reward for their toil. For if they fall, one will lift up his fellow; but woe to him who is alone when he falls and has not another to lift him up" (Eccl. 4:9-10). Of course, one of the greatest benefits of friendship is the encouragement, assistance, and support that a friend offers. Certainly, the Christian life and life in general contain many pitfalls, obstacles, and struggles. All of us from time to time find ourselves down and out, defeated, and discouraged. Sin, evil, and adverse circumstances occasionally seem to have the upper hand in our lives. If one is simply alone in such times, the weight of one's problems and personal failures can be crushing. Family members can indeed give great support – but only in so far as they are truly our friends. Yet even above the love of family stands the love of those to whom we have joined ourselves in freedom, those that we count as "second selves," who love us dearly, but are not bound to us by a multitude of practical and natural connections, as is the case with family. Thus we feel a certain freedom in sharing our struggles with our friends, knowing that they will hear, support, and love us apart from the inevitable anxieties and compromises wrought by family relationships.

In this role, genuine Christian friends are invaluable as counselors and advisors on the pathway of the kingdom. In Western cultures, pastors and spiritual fathers who have the understanding and time to function as true spiritual guides are quite rare. Yet there may be those outside of formal spiritual relationships who have much to offer for our spiritual growth: our friends. As fellow-pilgrims on the path of life eternal, their genuine care for our souls and knowledge of our hearts renders them particularly able to impart sagacious counsel to us. The benefit of having true companions on the road to life can hardly be overestimated. They will lift us up when we are down, encourage us when we are faint-hearted, cheer our noblest aspirations, challenge us when we become complacent, and comfort us when we sorrow.

The function of friends in offering reproof and correction is especially important. Few know us as well as our best friends. Major aspects of our personality may remain obscure even to close family members. But if we have truly opened our hearts to our friends, they understand us too well to allow us to fool them. Nor, if they are true friends, will they allow us to fool ourselves. When we need to be challenged, reminded of things we would prefer to forget, or called on the carpet for irresponsible behavior, godly Christian friends will do it. It is a bastardized notion of friendship that insists that a friend must approve all of one's actions. The sacred duty of virtuous friends is to recognize and reach out to us when we begin to go astray. Thus they may be compelled to speak hard words to us. Knowing that they know us as they do, it is difficult for us to evade or gainsay their loving reproof and correction.

Godly friends gain this privilege because they have demonstrated their willingness to listen to us and their ability to truly *hear* us. Our good friends do not merely desire to talk *to* us; they are interested in us and greatly desire to know us intimately. As we have discussed above, the result is *the conversation*, an experience of mutual revelation and understanding. Few spoken words are more difficult to bear than inept or misplaced advice. Our best friends are generally exempt from this liability, because they long ago demonstrated their proficiency at understanding us. They have heard us, understood us, and out of the storehouse of their wisdom have earned the right to reprove and correct us.

The facility of listening has benefits other than offering the right to reprove, however. It is a great source of consolation to know that there is one who is always ready to listen to the innermost stirrings of one's heart. How liberating it is to feel that there is always a friend to whom one may turn at any time with anything that happens to be occupying one's thoughts, whether joyous, sorrowful, amusing, thought-provoking, edifying, exciting, or just plain ordinary. There is one there that will hear and will care. That is the point.

The Creativity of Friendship

Because we allow our friends access to the intimate spaces of our hearts, we place them in a position to deeply affect us. This occurs in a wide variety of ways, but with regard to Christian life, it is vital to recognize how our friends stimulate our creativity. In particular, our friends play a crucial role in bringing to the fore aspects of our own selves of which we are only dimly aware. They elicit from us our unformed moral intimations, and through their dialogue with us, help us to forge them into distinct convictions and modes of practice. They discern and seize upon our deepest spiritual aspirations and encourage us to strive more mightily to realize them than we could ever do alone. They distinguish our weaknesses and temptations, and compassionately empower our resistance and triumph. They confirm and strengthen our faith. They recognize our genuine gifts and talents, and embolden the humble expression of them. They energize in us the establishment of new and beneficial habits. They help us realize our innate capacity to love.

Fundamentally, genuine friends grant us access to the most creative dimensions of our souls by receiving us and reflecting us back to ourselves. In this way, we are able to see what could not be seen before. We encounter our own identity and possibilities in fresh and dynamic ways. We can act in a manner previously unthinkable to us. Friends liberate our own inner resources for God's disposal, and thus are channels for the mediation of his grace to us. In Wadell's words, "So often our friends see in us a potential for goodness we cannot see ourself. Through their love for us, they bring unsuspected aspects of ourself to life. Or sometimes we see these possibilities but are not able to touch them. It does not matter. Our friends touch them, our friends draw them out of ourself. Through them we are put in touch with the deepest, most promising aspects of ourself. They lead us to discover ourself in ways we had not known before" (161).

In summary, godly friendships foster the development of our soul. They are the condition of possibility for our growth in virtue. Without them, it would be extremely difficult to progress on the path to deification. The realization of our person in the full image and likeness of God depends to a large degree on their companionship on our spiritual path. Wadell sums up this theme, "Friends are those who by being lovingly and patiently attentive to us make us into a person we could have never become on our own. Through their painstaking kindness, the studied ways they seek our good, through the artistry of their charity, they bring us into being. Friendship is creative, but it is the friends who create one another, bringing each other to life through the splendor of their love" (161).

Fruitful Friendships

The creative power of friendship is not limited to the friends themselves, however. Speaking of the self-transcending effect of love, Robert Spitzer writes, "Deep interpersonal unity becomes a living entity; our *me's* meld into an us. The relationship becomes an interpersonal person. When this degree of unity occurs in marriage or deep friendship, it becomes necessary for the friends or couple to find a common vision or shared cause larger than themselves, for a relationship, like an individual, much reach beyond itself or wither. There are many goods beyond 'ourselves': common projects or ideals, children, or the community, to name a few" (92, italics his).

Spitzer's point is that love relationships tend to "dead-end" when the focus of both persons is strictly on each other. This can be seen in marriages where couples consciously opt not to have children. The same effect can occur in friendships. Even when they purport to be grounded in virtue, they can become sterile when they fail to look beyond themselves to others. This is why deep Christian friendships often give birth to some form of ministry, whether prayer, social service, missionary or evangelistic activity, or building institutions. The love of the friends is grasped by the kingdom of God and thus moves beyond itself to be poured forth into others. Such friendships become spiritually fruitful.

Because they are profoundly energizing and spiritually creative, friendships offer rich possibilities for a full Christian life and profound growth in godliness. Nevertheless, they also present their own unique set of issues, problems and potential pitfalls. It is to these that we now turn our attention.

CHAPTER EIGHT

Issues and Problems in Friendships

Friendships undoubtedly arise from a wide variety of circumstances and embrace people from every walk of life. Yet if a friendship is going to attain a high degree of perfection, it must embody certain principles and avoid other perilous pitfalls.

The ancient Greek philosophers identified friendship based on virtue as its highest form. Friends who are engaged in the mutual pursuit of understanding, goodness, and ultimately, God, are drawing near to the core and center of all human existence and meaning. Yet few friendships originate in such an exalted quest. More often, they start with things like the discovery of a similar sense of humor or similar tastes in music. As we have discussed above, a friendship can be said to exist when the relationship moves beyond an occasional to a general experience of mutuality. From this develops the sense of unity of soul and the resultant intimate communion we have described.

Needs, Possessiveness, and Expectations

If perfect intimacy is to be attained and preserved in a friendship, however, certain basic principles must be honored. The first is the absolute necessity of maintaining *distance* in the relationship.[1] We may imagine that the common dimension shared by friends exists in the delicate space in between them.

It is also above, below, and around them, but especially between them.[2] This space is delicate because numerous forms of over-identification can collapse it, such as possessiveness, inappropriate expectations, involvement in mundane obligations, and sexual activity.

We have seen how solid friendship requires two persons that are fundamentally psychologically sound. The element of neediness on the part of one or the other is an inherently destabilizing force that seeks to obliterate the distance between the two. The needy person seeks to make the other perform a desired function within his own unhealthy psychic system. He thus must subjugate the friend and mold him into the role demanded by his needs. The other then is not encountered as a true person and is not allowed his full humanity. He exists as a role player in the inner world of the needy friend. The distance that must exist between two real people cannot abide because the needy one must wholly encompass the other to gain his required psychological fix. In other words, a friend plays out a largely symbolic function for the needy person, and thus cannot be allowed the freedom of a real person. A real person's distance from the needy one constitutes the possibility of a real life apart from his own, which the needy friend cannot tolerate.

In healthier persons, a less jaundiced approach to friendship can nonetheless bear similar traits when possessiveness begins to assert itself in the relationship. A person can become possessive of a friend out of intense love and devotion, because of a lack of other friends, as a result of personal insecurities, or out of a propensity toward controlling others. This can be differentiated from the extreme neediness described above, however, by the fact that the initial attraction to the friend is not based on disturbed functioning. However, in the course of the development of the friendship, tendencies toward possessiveness begin to assert themselves. Like the approach of the very needy, this possessiveness is also a movement to collapse the distance between the two, so that the other may exist as a function of oneself.[3] It is once again a denial of the friend's freedom and autonomy. Yet the freedom and autonomy of real persons are precisely the prerequisites of genuine friendship.

Expectations are the subtle fuel for the development of possessiveness in friendships. These must be clearly distinguished from necessary mutual commitments between friends. Ideally, the nature of these commitments is found in common ideals, values, and morals. These virtuous principles provide a firm base for the actual conduct of the relationship; one trusts the character of his friend and thus setting rules for his behavior is out of the question. On the other hand, friends do indeed act thoughtlessly, carelessly, and selfishly from time to time. This is to be expected anywhere in the normal course of human relations. But the point is that a friend is guilty of a true moral failure in such instances. He has violated the fundamental shared principles upon which the relationship has been built, and not just the expectations of the other.

The development of highly specific sets of expectations among friends is another matter altogether. At bottom, it betrays a lack of trust. It reveals the desire to regulate and control the other. It abandons high standards of virtue, freedom, and responsibility for the niggling restrictions of one's own conceptions of rectitude.

True friends relish the distance between them as much as the communion that unites them. This is because they recognize that the distance between free, whole, autonomous persons is the essential precondition of their relatedness. A sound friendship will repudiate every movement to collapse that distance by coercing the identity of one's friend into a function of one's own. As Paul Florensky puts it, "This unity is not a dissolution of individuality, not its depreciation, but its raising, consolidating, fortifying and deepening" (312). Accumulating expectations, tendencies toward possessiveness, attempts to control, and coercion by unbalanced needs are all poisonous to any potential or actual friendship. If friendship is to grow and to thrive, it can only do so in the fertile soil of freedom. Andrew Sullivan comments, "And like most truly free things, [friendship] does not conform to any simple purpose or direction. To ask what a friend is for is to mistake the nature of a friend. A friend is for herself and nothing else. If you enter a friendship to be less lonely, then it is not a friendship" (212).

Friendships and Business

Mutual involvement in mundane obligations also constitutes a grave threat to the health of friendships. The classic example is friends going into business together. We are all aware of the cliché that friends who wish to remain friends must never go into business with each other. Of course, friends are made in the workplace every day. The common activities and tasks provide a ready-made base of mutuality in which friendships quite naturally emerge. Yet the danger is that the accomplishment of tasks and the attainment of goals will become the priority in the relationship. The result may be that the friendship may not thrive under the coercion of business necessity. Fundamentally, common involvement in business injects a heavy dose of obligation and thus expectation into the relationship, and these are the enemies of the free relations of the friends. The friends cannot seek each other and experience each other purely for the joy of their friendship. They are subjected to the enterprise that sets the conditions of their relationship and rules over it.

Additionally, when money is at stake, disputes and disagreements are bound to arise. It takes a strong friendship, high ethical standards, excellent communication skills, good control over the passions, and the ability of both to reason carefully to avoid ruptures over the inevitable decisions that must be made. Beyond this, a great amount of tolerance for disagreement over substantial issues and the ability to forgive the mistakes and blunders of others are qualities that may be called upon frequently. Friendships among business partners are friendships in serious risk of dissolution.

Making friendships subservient to preoccupations other than virtue places an unnatural weight on them that they are not meant to bear. Sullivan describes the real function of friends, showing how alien to the concerns of business they are: "[Friendship] merely flourishes, a sign that human beings can choose one another for company, enjoy each other's selves, and accompany each other on an enterprise, with no thought of gain or purpose. In a utilitarian world, it is useless in the best sense of the word. It resists the meaning of anything but itself" (213).

Sex and Friendship

If common involvement in business is risky, sexual involvement between friends is deadly. Bodily union crushes that "delicate space" in between the two friends in which the friendship itself resides. Those who were formerly friends awaken from their indulgence in passion to find their relationship irreversibly altered by their acquiescence to *eros*. A new and heretofore foreign dimension of obligation has now intruded into the friendship, resulting in an entanglement that sacrifices personal distinctness to common identity. "Do you not know that he who joins himself to a prostitute becomes one flesh with her?" (1 Cor. 6:16).

Sexual desire is born of the need to consume another, to integrate her into one's own being. Nothing could be more opposite to the natural movement of friendship. For a friendship seeks not to obliterate the distinction between two persons, but to hold it intact while the dimension of communion grows between them. Sexual activity injects the role of biological determinism into a relationship; friendship seeks an experience of freedom unaffected by the constraints of nature. Of course, sexual relations involve a heavy dose of expectations, obligations, and possessiveness, all of which, as we have seen, are enemies of the freedom of friendship.

Friends therefore must be wary of eroticizing their relationship. This danger is especially real in male/female friendships, same sex friendships among those with homosexual inclinations, and in certain close friendships among women. The dynamics are the same in all three cases, although more obviously in the first two. Frequent association leading to increasing emotional intimacy, deepening affection and appreciation, a growing experience of unity and communion, and physical expressions such as hugging and caressing all may conspire to awaken a sense of yearning and desire that moves beyond the affectionate to the erotic. The love becomes sexualized and passes beyond *philia* into *eros*. When this occurs, it seems that physical union with the other would be the most natural expression and fulfillment of one's love. One desires to encompass, consume, internalize, and merge with the other. The creative tension that keeps distance between friends while cultivating communion begins to collapse. Bodies come together, and the creative distance that upholds friendship is crushed.

Friends then awaken from a sexual encounter with the subtle sense or perhaps brutal realization that everything is different. Do they now belong to each other? Must they forsake marriages and other relationships? Will they have sex again (and again and again)? Will they set up housekeeping with one another? Will one party expect more sex against the wishes of the other? Have they fallen into sin, and thus has shame now entered their friendship? Can it ever be what it was before? Is the friendship now to be a perpetual locus of temptation? Unconscious dynamics unleashed by biology now assert themselves against the freedom of the friendship.

Understanding these processes reveals why the notion of "platonic" relationships is not a matter of repression and denial of authenticity, as if acting out sexually is the highest form of honesty and truth when desire begins to assert itself. Rather, the platonic relationship means maintaining an ideal and being unwilling to allow it to be corrupted or compromised by forces inalienably hostile to friendship.

As stated above, the danger for cross-gender (male/female) friendships and those among the homosexually inclined is obvious. But why particularly among female friendships as opposed to male friendships? This is because some friendships among women thrive on a high degree of emotional connection, and women's sexual desires often arise directly from such a sense of emotional connection. "Guy" friendships often involve mutual interests and activities (cars, sports, intellectual pursuits) and by nature are much more aloof. Women are generally more comfortable with physical expressions of affection among themselves, while men are uneasy with them. The result is that female friendships can more readily be eroticized: emotional connection coupled with physical expressions of affection may result in erotic desire and indulgence. This is especially a temptation where close female friends have had continual disappointments in relationships with men. Such disappointment leads to hostility and resentment and the belief that only female bonding can be satisfying. These friends allow erotic desire to capture their friendship and then may begin to identify themselves as "lesbians."

Friendship in Marriage

The inherent conflict between *philia* and *eros* explains the problem of friendship in marriage. We are all aware of the phenomenon where two long-term friends find themselves "falling in love." Soon they set up housekeeping or get married, only to find that their friendship seems to be disappearing. They are puzzled and mystified. Shouldn't they even be closer now that they are living together and sharing their lives?

The problem is explained easily by what we have discussed above: the collapse of distance brought about by involvement in sex and the business of day-to-day obligations. This is why *differentiation* is a critical concept in marital relations. Psychologist David Schnarch defines it as follows, *"[D]ifferentiation is your ability to maintain your sense of self when you are emotionally and/or physically close to others – especially as they become increasingly important to you* . . . Differentiation is the ability to stay in connection without being consumed by the other person" (56, italics his). Each spouse needs to maintain a strong sense of personal identity for a genuine *relationship* to exist. Otherwise, spouses may tend to reduce their mates to functionaries, either in the sense of someone who is there to fulfill practical obligations, or someone who has become an extension of one's own identity. Only when spouses are well-differentiated, that is, have interests, friendships, activities, hobbies, jobs, ideas, and roles that are unique and distinct from each other's, is there enough distance in the relationship for friendship to survive. Unquestionably, in some marriages it not only survives, but thrives. This only occurs where spouses are careful to maintain their unique identities, and thus can remain authentically selves-in-relation.

Gender and Friendship

Consideration of friendship in marriage leads us to the

broader issue of cross-gender friendships in general. There is no question that this phenomenon represents a special "problem" in the arena of friendships. The reason is obvious and can be placed in the form of a simple question: Can friendship be maintained between the opposite sexes without contamination by sexual desire? To this query we may add one even more basic: Can a man and a woman really be friends?

There are those who seem ready to answer in the negative. C.S. Lewis asserts "the sexes will have met in Affection and Eros, but not in this love" (105). But it quickly becomes apparent that his only reason for denying it is that he sees that men and women do not intermingle freely enough for the formation of friendships. He realizes that there are certain professions in which this is not the case, and imagines a world in which such would be possible. Writing in England in the 1950's, however, he hardly could have imagined the fluidity of the association between the sexes in the West at the dawn of the 21st century.

Westerners live in cultures in which men and women interact and work side by side in all walks of life. In this setting, it is natural not only that romances will develop and that sexual misconduct will be rife, but that friendships will emerge between men and women. Such relationships seem inevitable in the modern setting. Yet this is an area in which great caution ought be exercised. It seems indisputable in most cases, that cross-gender friendships cannot be conducted in the same relaxed and carefree manner as same-gender friendships. In many cases, they probably can only be pursued in limited and restrictive contexts. Nonetheless, moralizing and admonishment will not stop them from happening.[4] Our task is to understand and describe the dynamics involved with them, especially with regard to the relationship between *philia* and *eros*.

Andrew Sullivan and C.S. Lewis both emphasize that common gender provides a basic commonality that readily grounds friendship. But while same-sex friendships are undoubtedly easier and more common, this tells us nothing about the real possibility for male/female friendship. Sullivan notes that such friendships are "always subject to the destabilizing force of love," by which he means *eros*. He notes that if they are to work out, male/female friends must "put the temptation of eros behind them . . ." (207). Lewis, too, describes various scenarios in which such friendships can flourish and how *eros* may impact them (98-100).

Without going into overmuch detail, we may recognize that *eros* can create problems in certain cross-gender friendships, namely, when at least one of the friends is married or in a highly committed relationship. Otherwise, if *eros* develops between two single people who are friends, it is only a problem in so far as temptations to illicit sexual contact arise between them and threaten the dynamics of their friendship. It may complicate the relationship, but the presence of *eros* itself, the love that is desire, does not present an insuperable problem for two unattached singles.

The development of romance would in fact constitute a serious problem for friendships in which one or both parties are married or in a highly committed relationship. Again, it must be emphasized that it is difficult to imagine most such friendships being conducted other than in a highly restricted context. To highlight the issues involved, we may imagine friendships functioning in several different scenarios: first, where no physical attraction exists at all; second, where some physical attraction exists on the part of one or both parties, but no desire for sexual contact or fantasizing; third, when definite physical attraction on the part of one or both has resulted in desire and fantasy. Of course, these are not rigid categories, and certainly relationships have segued from the first through the third and beyond. But considering these different scenarios in cross-gender relationships will be helpful for our purposes.

In the first case, where there is no physical attraction, it is hard to see why a friendship should not be engaged and maintained. There is no substantial reason why closeness and friendship between a man and a woman should be considered morally suspect in itself. Certainly, the warnings imbedded in the venerable ascetical tradition must be taken seriously. But the issue there is always the danger of falling into sexual temptation. Yet as long as there is no attraction or desire involved, what is the problem? Some men and women seem to be capable of being good friends with each other without ever being drawn toward anything more than that. Outside of temptations, is there something inherently reprehensible about a man and a woman understanding one another and enjoying each other's company outside of marriage?

Such is only the case if we sexualize any kind of intimacy. This mentality is not uncommon, even to the point where close friendships among the same sex become suspect as forms of "homosexuality" (see Lewis, 90-91). From a Christian point of view, this outlook is questionable, in that it identifies human beings first and foremost as potential objects of sexual desire rather than as persons. A true male/female friendship reasserts the essential primacy of the person, created in the image and likeness of God, over an approach that prioritizes the sexual dynamics of every cross-gender encounter. The latter is not done by only the lustful and libertines. Systemic institutionalization of the phenomenon can be seen in certain forms of Islamic and Christian fundamentalism. Women in particular are treated as the embodiment of human sexual temptation that must be cloistered and controlled at all costs. The possibility of a genuine relationship between a man and a woman as persons is disallowed from the outset (see note above). Such a view primarily tends to depersonalize women for men, but the reverse can also occur. It errs in that it fails to make any distinction between *eros* and *philia* on one hand, and establishes a false primacy of gender over human nature. These positions are not compatible with the fundamental Christian principles we have outlined above.

What about when some sense of attraction is present? It is possible to recognize that another person is attractive without falling into lustful fantasies. To be sure, when desire or fantasy begins to rear its head, the possibility for honest friendship is diminished. It is at this point that the manner in which a male/female friendship is conducted is of critical importance. Spending time alone together in private settings, conversation with explicit romantic or sexual overtones, a great deal of "innocent" touching, all serve to stimulate desire and fantasy. Thus, while I would affirm the possibility for friendship to exist between two "attractive" members of the opposite sex, it must be conducted with extreme modesty and reserve. Otherwise, good fellowship may end up being replaced by a state of continual temptation.

A cross-gender friendship in the third situation can no longer be a friendship in a meaningful sense. The desire of one or both parties now is moving to collapse the distance in which friendship dwells, and to consummate a union of the flesh. The soul-boundary has been crossed and the physical boundary will follow, unless there is determined resistance on the part of one friend. The relationship now exists as a continual stimulus to passion and desire. Although it still may be a friendship in some sense, the dynamics have moved beyond friendship's parameters. An untenable state exists which can only be resolved by the hard decision to terminate the relationship.

Unless the friends have the courage to leave it behind, it will end up in adultery and/or the catastrophic disruption of other important ties. There is only one way for cross-gender friendships to succeed if there is attraction involved. This is by means of the ancient principle of sublimation, as described by Plato centuries ago. Gilbert Meilaender comments on Plato's teaching as follows: "The unruly steed (*eros*) can be disciplined and controlled only over a period of time. If this is achieved, what began in *eros* will end in *philia*. Eros without gratification means for the lovers a shared life in the pursuit of wisdom. When *eros* is sublimated, the lovers are able to recognize its character as sign and call and enabled to move beyond it to that to which it points. In this way *eros* leads to philosophy; lover and beloved now share in the love of wisdom. Indeed, friendship at its best consists in a shared love of wisdom, and for Plato *philia* is the end result of sublimated *eros*" (11).

In the Christian setting, this means that a cross-gender friendship can only be realized in the context of an inner asceticism that refuses to yield to passion out of the yearning for something greater than sexual satisfaction. For the friendship to succeed, it is not necessary to deny that sexual tension may exist. The legitimacy of the relationship does not depend on a total absence of *eros*, rather, it depends on whether *eros* can be transformed by sublimation into true *philia*. Psychologically, there is no doubt that this is possible; there is also no doubt that the path is difficult. The risks must be soberly considered and the necessary boundaries must be firmly observed. Again, this requires inner ascetical disciplines such as watchfulness, the discerning of thoughts, and control over tendencies to fantasy. The reward, however, is greater than promised by Plato. It is not only wisdom, but communion with each other and God in the Holy Spirit.

We do find classic examples in the Christian tradition of the pairing of men and women in the spiritual life outside of marriage. Church history reveals the story of Paul and Thecla, the poignant relationship between John Chrysostom and Olympias, the deep affection between Jerome and Paula, and the controversial practices regarding the *"agapetae"* or *"virgines subintroductae."*[5] In Russian spirituality, close relations between abbots and abbesses of nearby monasteries are not uncommon, and the relationship between Francis of Assisi and Clare and Francis de Sales and Jeanne de Chantal are well-known Roman Catholic examples. These relationships were forged in a context of celibacy and asceticism that is not readily transferable to those in the world. Nevertheless, the potential for temptation certainly cannot be less for the celibate than for those who have other outlets for the expression of *eros*.

Ultimately, we may conclude that male/female friendships centered in Christian life can be legitimate and are defensible. They may be rare. Temptation may potentially lurk in the shadows. They definitely require great care, self-control, watchfulness and discipline. Yet we must hold out for the possibility of friendships in which men and women do not depersonalize each other into objects of desire, but relate precisely and fully as persons to persons. These are relationships that forge the transformation of *eros* into a glorious and rich *philia*. They reclaim the truth that the fundamental human reality is the one nature we share in the image and likeness of God, to which gender is subsidiary.

Friendships and Balance

In much contemporary marriage and family psychology, it is often assumed that spouses should be all things to each other. It is as if every conceivable human need and desire should be met within the context of marriage. This notion, however, places entirely too much weight on a marriage. As Sullivan observes, "Families and marriages fail too often because they are trying to answer too many human needs. A spouse is required to be a lover, a friend, a mother, a father, a soul-mate, a co-worker, and so on. Few people can be all these things for one person . . . If husbands and wives have deeper and stronger friendships outside the marital unit, the marriage has more space to breathe and fewer burdens to bear" (234).

Sullivan sees that this same force may also work to endanger friendships. When too much weight is placed on them, friendships will likewise suffer. "If we have many friends and no real family, we tend to demand of friends things which are equally inappropriate – the need-love and deep security that only lovers and parents and spouses can provide" (234). This is even truer when a person has few, or perhaps even one, close friendships and no family. When a friendship must bear the weight of all one's needs and desires, as we observed above, the distance required for a healthy relationship collapses and the relationship will not endure.

Marriage partners cannot be everything to each other; their interests, desires, and pursuits can never be identical. Spouses therefore derive great benefit from other friendships in which they can express these aspects of their personalities. Furthermore, the distance between friends frequently may allow a married person a greater sense of ease in talking with a friend about certain subjects that might arouse an emotional reaction in a spouse. A friend can often be a great listener, because he does not bring the same level of emotional involvement to the situation as a spouse would.[6]

Friendships are vitally important in the overall balance of human relationships. A human being without a true friend is a person in peril. But any given friendship cannot sustain the friends by itself. The pressure can become too great and the intimacy suffocating. Chains of bondage may overcome the freedom of the relationship.

Suffering and Friendship

Even if one avoids placing ultimate weight on friendships, it is inevitable that our friends will bring us sorrow as well as joy.[7] Whether it is the sadness brought on by accidental circumstances, such as illness, financial setbacks, physical injuries, relocation, or finally death, it is certain that our love for our friends will be a source of pain. This is even more the case when there are difficulties or even a rupture in the relationship. Paul Wadell describes it with typical eloquence: "What is remarkable about the moral life is not that morality is friendship, but that all our friends were once our strangers. What is remarkable about friends is what a risk it is to let a stranger become one. But we take that risk. No matter how many times we might be hurt, even betrayed, by those to whom we risked ourselves, we continue to take a chance with them because intuitively we know that we cannot abide a self without them" (148).

Those who venture into deep friendship count this exposure and vulnerability entirely worth the price of the friend's love. Paul Florensky quotes a poem found in a friend's dairy and includes his friend's comment:

"If you wish to live without struggle, without storm,
Without knowing the bitterness of life, to ripe old age,
Do not seek a friend and do not call yourself anyone's friend.
You will taste fewer joys, but also fewer sorrows!"

"Yes, but the important thing here is this 'if.' In my opinion, not only is the rhythmic alternation of grief and joy with a friend infinitely more valuable than an even and peacefully flowing life in solitude, but I would not even trade con-

THE FEAST OF FRIENDSHIP

tinuous grief with a friend for continuous solitary joy" (324). What greater testimony to the power of suffering friendship could be conceived?

Florensky also notes how the unity of soul between friends lends suffering an entirely different character than it would have in other circumstances. "Friendship involves not co-rejoicing and co-suffering, but rather the more profound states of consonant rejoicing and consonant suffering. The states of the former type go from the periphery of the soul to its center and refer to those who are comparatively more remote from us. But the joy and suffering of those who are very close to us, arising in the very center of our soul, are directed from there to the periphery: this is not the reflection of an alien state, but of one's own consonant state, one's own joy and one's own suffering" (311). The joys and sufferings of a friend become purely one's own, without distinction. It is natural to affirm this in the case of joy; friendship has achieved itself when it is just as true of suffering. If empathy is defined as a direct participation in the ideas and feelings of another, then the shared sense of suffering common to friends and loved ones is its epitome.

Moral failings and acts of betrayal place a strain on friendships that ultimately may be too great to bear. Such failings may be major or minor; they may involve both friends or others. They may be a direct affront to one's friend or to the common principles and values upon which the friendship is founded. But in any such case, the friendship has suffered an assault. In this situation, only one thing can bring healing and restoration: forgiveness. Friends must be willing to forgive friends if they are to remain friends. If there is no forgiveness, the friendship has been based on an impossible ideal that it could never fulfill. We must recognize, however, that in some cases the betrayal has been so grave that it is even beyond the reach of forgiveness. The offended friend may indeed forgive, but the friendship has been damaged to the point where trust has been destroyed and the relationship is beyond repair. In such cases, it is terminated. There is no other option.

Our friendships embody all the mystery and adventure that life is. They challenge us with a multitude of problems even as they offer us a fullness that, once tasted, we cannot live without. They deliver joy beyond words and suffering beyond calculation. In spite of how they may hurt us, having entered into them, we are never the same again. Our friends have become an inalienable part of us and we of them. We have drunk deeply of their souls and they of ours. Except for perhaps our marriages, families, and our relationship with God, nothing that life offers brings us greater fulfillment.

8 Notes

1. Sullivan is among other writers who describe this phenomenon, without elevating it to a formal concept as I have done. See his discussion of the difference between friendship and love (*eros*), (209-211).

2. Paul Florensky hints at such a "spatialization" of the relations between friends: "One feels, desires, thinks, and speaks not because the other spoke, thought, desired, or felt in the same way, but because both feel one feeling, desire with one will, think one thought, speak with one voice. Each lives by the other, or rather, the life of the one and the other flow from a common center, one in itself, placed by the friends above themselves by a creative act" (311).

3. William Lynch aptly describes how true communion demands that each friend possesses autonomy and a solid identity: "When there is maturity in and love between two people, there is no confusion. There are closeness, strong ties, a mixing without confusion of personalities, feelings, wishes. Ideally they feel for each other and wish with each other. So far as we can judge, the reason such closeness is possible without confusion is that each is an independently existing person . . . They may and indeed do have common feelings, but each also knows that the common feeling is his or her feeling, a genuine internally possessed feeling. The same is true for their wishes when they are common, close and united . . . the wish is also separately and genuinely present in each. There is a degree in their separate identities which gives them a certain ease in allowing a close

relationship to grow" (92). Interestingly, Paul Florensky gives a positive interpretation of jealousy in friendship which he distinguishes from what I have described as possessiveness: "Suspiciousness, hate with envy, and so forth are all bad, reprehensible, egotistical *manifestations* of jealousy, produced by the confusion of love with desire" (334). He asserts, however, that jealousy itself is "one of the aspects of love, the foundation of love, the background of love, the primordial darkness in which love shines." He derives its fundamental importance in friendship from his conviction that true friendship is limited to two persons, each of whom becomes a *complete* Thou for the other. In this there can be no others; no rivals can be tolerated (see 335).

4. The classic Orthodox manual on the spiritual life, *Unseen Warfare*, contains the following ascetical instructions: "The rule here is to avoid all occasions which may upset the calm of your body, especially meeting people of the opposite sex. If you are forced to converse with such a person, let the conversation be short, and preserve not only modesty but a certain sternness of countenance; let your words be friendly, but reserved rather than forthcoming" (119). The context, of course, presumes that the protagonist is celibate and probably a monastic. The advice is certainly sensible for that situation and many others. If taken too far, however, the possibility of sexual temptation then completely constitutes the relations between man and woman, so that the experience of their common humanity in the image of God is obviated. While giving our fallen nature its due, if a man and a woman cannot relate as persons, as friends, in Christ, a tragic situation truly exists. Much ascetical literature, primarily ancient, simply demonizes women as a source of temptation. Although in that context it makes practical sense, this can never be the Christian standard because it is inherently dehumanizing. To justify the depersonalization of women on

account of male lust is abhorrent. The Taliban regime in Afghanistan is sufficient example.

5. Peter Brown's *The Body and Society* traces the outlines of such relationships in the context of late antique concepts of the body and sexuality. (On Paula and Thecla in particular, see 155-159). The *Agapetae* were virgins who consecrated themselves to God with a vow of chastity and lived with laymen for material support and common spiritual life. It is probable that these virgins, who did not live in community, required men to take care of their material needs, and thus they naturally connected with those who had likewise taken vows of chastity. Of course, the practice resulted in abuses and scandals, and it was condemned by several councils of the fourth century. *Virgines subintroductae* were women who lived with clerics without marriage. The practice was likewise condemned. The condemnations, however, did not stop these practices from being widespread and common. Brown's succinct comment is that "Female spiritual friends and protégées were branded as *suneisaktai* in Greek or *subintroductae* in Latin, 'call-in girls' and also *agapetae*, 'love-birds.' They stood for a disturbing category of permanent companionship with a man who was neither father, brother, nor husband to them" (267). Although the appropriateness and sense of such relationships is highly questionable and the probability of succumbing to tempation extreme, we must acknowledge that in all likelihood, some such relationships were indeed chaste and holy.

6. See Sullivan, (214-5) for elaboration of this point.

7. See Wadell, (154) for further discussion.

CHAPTER NINE

Psychological Considerations

In our initial reflections, we briefly noted some of the most basic psychological factors involved in friendships. Having grounded our view of friendship in the Orthodox theological tradition and considered its interpersonal processes, it is time to further explore the psychological forces at work in friendships.

In discussing the parameters of friendship, we touched on some of the unhealthy dynamics that create problems for friends. Beyond these considerations, however, it is useful to examine some of the elemental unconscious forces that drive friendships. In doing so, I will make use of generalized and simplified concepts drawn from Jungian psychology. This is not because Jung is the last word in psychology; rather, it is simply that some of his basic insights are helpful for our purpose.

We have noted that one of the most ancient and durable metaphors for friendship is "one soul in two bodies." We have discussed the factors that form this experience and pointed toward its spiritual dimensions. Yet we have not examined why two particular individuals awaken to this precisely with *each other*, other than to note the discovery of mutual interests and views. But surely more than this is required for the development of the astounding sense of oneness that characterizes the closest of friendships.

What occurs between two people when this experience of soul-unity develops? Upon what does it rest? What processes underlie it? We have seen that a spiritual foundation exists in the unity of humanity in the one Christ. But this hardly explains everything. It must also have a psychological basis, since it is rooted in the mind and heart of real persons. The suggestions that follow are based on psychological themes that may have some bearing on these questions.

Type and Friendships

First, an empirical basis for the sense of unity between friends may be found in similarity of *type*. Jung identified four primary psychic functions in addition to the basic orientations of introversion and extraversion. From this he developed a system of personality types that subsequently was used as the basis for professional evaluative instruments such as the Myers-Briggs Temperament Indicator and other similar tests. Although scorned by some as "intellectual voodoo,"[1] and likened by others to astrology and other forms of superstition, Myers-Briggs has enjoyed wide popularity for decades and continues to be employed in counseling and professional human resource settings.

With regard to marriage, type theory operates on the Jungian assumption that "opposites attract;"[2] that is, that one seeks a partner who embodies the traits lacking in one's self. Thus, an introverted intuitive thinking judging type (INTJ) is likely to be attracted to an extraverted sensate feeling perceiving type (ESFP). One completes oneself by the choice of a partner whose characteristics are complimentary rather than identical to one's own.

If the preponderant element in close friendships is a sense of similarity rather than complementarity, however, we may surmise that one source of the experience of unity may be *similarity of temperament.* One discovers another who thinks, feels, judges, and has habits nearly identical to one's own. The result is that empathy develops easily and naturally, allowing one seemingly to participate in the other's thoughts and feelings. This may also explain much of the phenomenon of "synchronicity" that occurs between friends: uncanny correspondences in thought, feeling, choices, and activities that almost seem "psychic" in nature. The basis for such experiences may lie partially in the fact that two people's temperaments are "hardwired" in a nearly identical way.

Not all friendships are of the "identity" type, however. Some are distinctly complimentary. In such cases, it is usually an external interest or activity that forges the bond of unity between the friends. Although they may have wide areas of agreement in taste and outlook, and share a deep affection for one another, some consciousness of the acute differences between them usually remains in focus. Thus such friends do not typically experience "unity of soul" in the way others do whose temperaments are quite alike.

Friendship: A Form of Self-love?

If the experience of unity and empathy between close friends is based to a large degree on similarity of type and temperament, this fact gives fresh impetus to an old problem. If what one loves in a friend is actually his similarity to oneself, is one then not loving oneself in the guise of a friend? Is such love then anything less than pure narcissism? Kierkegaard raised this issue two centuries ago in his critique of friendship.[3] He held that *philia* is inherently unchristian and unworthy for this reason.

What, then, takes places when one sees in a friend the mirror of one's own soul and feels strong love for the friend as a result? Is one simply loving oneself? Those who have had the experience must agree that there is a tremendous feeling of affirmation when one finds another who thinks and feels in a nearly identical manner. Why?

One explanation for the phenomenon of experiencing a friend as a "second self" might be that one projects aspects of his unconscious on to another so that he experiences only himself in the other. Thus what he loves in the friend is himself – the essence of Kierkegaard's criticism. In a completely blind projection, this may be true. This, however, is not the case in true friendship, where *differentiation* and *distance* are essential elements. Such projection cannot co-exist with these. In a genuine friendship, one finds one's core identity reflected, regarded and loved by another. But all along, one continues to notice the friend's own unique personal characteristics. Thus when one experiences soul-unity in this way, the primary reaction is not "how wonderful I am," or even "how wonderful my friend is," but "how wonderful this friendship is." It is precisely the unity in the face of the irreducible differences that is the marvel. Indeed, there is a commonality that is valued and esteemed. But it is valued and esteemed as it exists *in another*. Self is not completely out of view, but only in view in so far as one's identity has been unveiled through the *relatedness* inherent in friendship. One finds oneself in another and another in oneself. We have seen that one only becomes truly a person in relation to others. It is not narcissistic self-absorption that friendship promotes, but *communion*. This is unity-in-distinction, oneness of nature in a diversity of persons.

Thus what occurs psychologically in friendship reflects what we have described theologically. It is not narcissism for the Father to love the Son, though they are one in all respects save their hypostases. It is communion. The same principle holds for the deep love between friends. Communion is an experience of realizing essential commonality between persons in their hypostatic diversity. It is not to idolize oneself in the face of another; it is to realize oneself in relation to another and to find another in the depths of one's self.

The desire for communion is innate and essential to being human. We are what we were created to be when giving and receiving love. To answer Kierkegaard: yes, in this world, the practice of unrequited agape is essential to the Christian life. But one cannot survive on agape alone. We share vital loves within our families, and in addition to that, the *philia* between friends deepens and enriches love's place in our lives. It does not matter if it is experienced within the confines of the fixed social hierarchies of traditional societies or in the fluid and free associations characteristic of modern Western culture. Friendships realize the vital communion of love given and received.

The Unconscious and Archetypes

Another issue regarding friendships is the role of unconscious factors in constituting these relationships. The concern here is not with pathological motivations that we have previously mentioned, but with "normal" processes that may be involved in any such close relationship.

We noted above that we are hardly aware of all that motivates us in any relationship, friendships included. Soul-friendships in particular are a rich source for the investigation of unconscious processes because of the unusually deep attachments they foster. Apart from conscious features that can be readily identified, how do two people become so profoundly attached to each other? Beyond surface factors, what enamors them with each other?

Several elements merit consideration in this regard. First and most simply, a friend may embody a characteristic that is seemingly absent or only latent in oneself. Without recognizing explicitly why, one is moved to admire the friend and holds him in high esteem. In this case, he embodies or has achieved something that is largely unrealized in oneself, which in some instances may be a repressed aspiration that is mostly unconscious. For example, a certain heroic quality may accrue to an athletic friend if one is at heart a frustrated athlete.

Similarly, a friend may constellate or catalyze certain unconscious processes in oneself in such a way that one's unconscious then objectifies such contents by projecting them on to the friend. In such a case, the friend begins to function symbolically in one's psyche more significantly than as a literal social figure. An example would be where a female friend begins to take on a "glow" to a man and suddenly appears beautiful in a new and unforeseen way. The friend's appearance has not changed; rather, Eros has been activated and has projected a goddess-like aura on the woman. Jung held that in such a case a man's "anima" has projected itself upon the woman.

Unconscious processes can characterize friendships in such a way that a generalized transference becomes inherent in the relationship. This occurs, for instance, when one friend assumes a parental role in a friendship. In such cases, the friendship may appear "normal" and typical of deep friendships in general. Were one to look deeper, however, one would find that special roles, rules, and rituals govern the relationship. It is obvious that one is "up" and one is "down;" one is the "parent" and one is the "child." Such transferences in friendships are of necessity mutual though unconscious agreements about each one's place and functioning.

A still deeper form of unconscious activity takes place when a friend truly becomes the bearer of mythic significance.

This happens when a friend embodies an archetypal image for another. One's unconscious may bestow upon a friend the identity of a "knight in shining armor," a wise sage, a pure virgin, a conquering hero, a mystic sister, and many other such archetypal roles. Because of this, the relationship becomes invested with an overpowering and intense psychic force. One relates to the friend as the bearer of symbolic significance far beyond what the actual person warrants.

A relevant personal example derives from the experience of being a priest. It is quite easy to tell that many people relate to you as a priest symbolically with near-total disregard of your actual personhood. For some, a priest may be a Christ-figure who is thus invested with all kinds of messianic qualities. For others, a priest becomes an image of their own struggle with guilt. As a priest, it is certainly interesting to observe the ways the archetypal significance of the priest-image governs how most people relate to you, with little concern for your actual concrete humanity. Yet the occurrence of such processes need not be considered a completely negative phenomenon. As we shall see, an important symbolic role played by a friend in one's life may be vital to personal integration and wholeness.

The recognition that unconscious factors are active in some friendships does not mandate a cynical attitude or paint a gloomy picture. They may have a healthful and life-giving side. A friend may be an invaluable companion in the ascesis of one's soul work. His symbolic presence may awaken one to his own deepest needs and aspirations, which beforehand may have been only scarcely conscious. The objectification of unconscious contents through projection may lead to valuable insights about one's own psychic make-up, and prefigure one's transformation through the conscious integration of those contents.

Childlikeness and Symbolic Functions

For this to occur, a free and natural flow must characterize the relations between friends. A certain "childlikeness" is required. Jung pointed out the childlike character of a redeeming symbol: "The nature of the redeeming symbol is that of a child . . . childlikeness or lack of prior assumptions is the very essence of the symbol and its function. This childlike attitude necessarily brings with it another guiding principle in place of self-will and rational intentions" (i.e., typical adult forms of activity) (262). If this is true, then assimilation of the symbol's effect requires a similar attitude.

In friendships, this means that the symbolic function of a friend can act naturally upon one to elicit a corresponding childlike attitude in which one finds oneself feeling and acting in a natural, uncomplicated manner free from overt intentions. A transforming power grips and draws one's soul into a natural movement that seeks nothing other than the possibility of wholeness represented by the relationship with the friend. It is childlike in that it is unselfconscious and joyous. New and unforeseen possibilities emerge, rife with life's power. As Jung puts it, "In psychological terms, the functions that have lain fallow and unfertile, and were unused, repressed, undervalued, despised, etc., suddenly burst forth and begin to live" (263). It is patently obvious that such cannot occur if one is directed only by rational intentions and is continually consciously self-analytical. True friendships naturally tend to cultivate the atmosphere of childlikeness that allows symbolic functions to exercise their transformative potential.

However, a childlike attitude need not require submersion of adult awareness and an affected simplicity which pretends not to notice the psychological dynamics operative in a friendship. Rather, awareness of these pyschodynamics prevents one from falling completely under their sway and completely mythologizing the friend into a hero, god, or goddess. A psychologically aware friend can sense it when his own unconscious begins to play tricks on him, turning a friend into something more than his role warrants. He can choose to work with those dynamics for the sake of insight, or, seeing them, not take them too seriously. He can remain playful and natural in the face of such awareness because he is alive to the possibilities opened up by the symbolic functions inherent to the friendship, but refuses the temptation to take them literally and over-seriously.[4]

Ronald Rolheiser uses Paul Ricouer's concept of "second naivete" to describe this attitude. Speaking of development from childhood to adulthood, he writes, "Beyond the loss of natural naivete and natural contemplativeness (of a child) lies another kind of naivete and another kind of awareness, second naivete, the awareness which returns us to the posture of a child, which sees again with the directness of a child, but has now integrated into that posture the critical and practical concerns of an adult" (160). "Second naivete" then does not demand an artificial regression into a feigned childishness, but an adult experience of fundamental openness to mystery and realities beyond the definable and intentional. "A truly contemplative consciousness, one that is truly attuned to the full depth and mystery within reality, not only *wonders-how* but it especially *wonders-at* and wonders-at things when one has the eyes, the mind, and the heart of a child and virgin" (159, italics his). Rolheiser calls this process "revirginisation" and elaborates on it as follows: "Revirginisation refers to a process of continually recapturing the posture of a child before reality while second naivete describes that posture as it exists in an adult who has already moved beyond the natural naivete of a child but who is not fixated in the deserts of cynicism, criticism, and false sophistication" (159).

In a psychology of friendship, this means that although there is an adult side that can be aware of the psychodynamics operating in the friendship, a genuinely childlike experience is nonetheless still possible. This is a childlike posture beyond adult awareness that experiences the friendship in a natural and uncomplicated way. Thus a friend may have a highly symbolic function in one's psyche, and one may be aware of it. Yet more engaging than this knowledge is the sense of openness, mystery, depth and love in the friendship. The stance of a friend before these phenomena in awe and gratitude enables the relationship to go forward naturally and in freedom. One may have a sense of the power of a friend's symbolic role, and yet watch its effect unfold in oneself in a natural and unselfconscious way. On one hand, the awareness of unconscious psychological patterns might seem complicating and overly self-conscious. On the other hand, this knowledge sets one free from becoming the prey of forces that might otherwise dominate the dynamics of the relationship and thus disrupt its integrity.

Ultimately, a friendship is a relationship of love between persons who find a natural element of communion between them. It takes place largely on a conscious level, but unconscious forces are powerfully active within it. When such unconscious forces meet compatibly in two people, the dynamism of the relationship far exceeds what can be accounted for consciously. Behind the "collective consciousness" of a deep friendship lies a far more profound "collective unconscious" which forms and characterizes the peculiar relationship that each friendship is.

9 Notes

1. See David Mills, "Close Your Mind – Critical Christians in an Uncritical Age" in *Touchstone*, vol. 13, no. 8, October 2000, (25).

2. See Keirsey & Bates, *Please Understand Me*, (67-70) for a discussion of the principle. Unfortunately, the authors disparage Jung's rather convincing argument that marriage partners seek their opposite in order to complete themselves.

3. "The beloved and the friend are therefore called, remarkably and significantly enough, the *other*-self, the *other*-I . . . But wherein lies this self-love? It lies in the I, in the self. Would not self-love still remain in loving the other-self, the other-I?" (See Pakaluk, 241, italics his).

4. I have here modified the Jungian concept of "withdrawing the projection." It is not so much that the projected content must be realized and then repudiated, as that once it is seen, it can serve as a pathway to self-understanding. In the natural, childlike setting of a good friendship, this is not taken over-seriously. One's self-awareness grows happily, and paradoxically, unselfconsciously.

CHAPTER TEN

The Feast of Friendship

During our consideration of friendship, one theme has repeatedly come to the fore: deep friendship presses beyond itself to embody and reflect transcendent realities. The friendship relationship is itself transcendental. Its reality is greater than the "sum total" of the personalities of the individual friends. The union between friends' souls is an overarching dimension that subsumes and incorporates them while constituting itself in them. As such, it reflects the incorporation of distinct human persons into the transcendental dimension of Christ's glorified body. Furthermore, the communion of unique human persons in the one human nature of the new Adam is an image of the Holy Trinity, the Ground of all being, which is itself communion.

The Feast of the Kingdom

Just as the experience of friendship points to the most profound levels of being and relationship, so too it anticipates the definitive fulfillment of humanity. It is not only a revelation of the nature of Being, but a disclosure of the final destiny of human history. Christians call this ultimate realization the kingdom of God. In the kingdom, every human relationship attains its final perfection. God's kingdom is in fact a state of perfect interrelatedness among all persons in the hypostatic unity of the God-man Jesus Christ.

The Gospels represent the glorious kingdom in a wealth of images and symbols. A familiar metaphor for the kingdom in the parables of Jesus is that of a banquet or wedding feast (Luke 14:14-24, Matt. 22:1-14, 25:1-13). In the Synoptic accounts of the Last Supper, Jesus envisions the kingdom as a reunion of friends feasting at the table. Taking the cup, he tells them "I say to you, I will not drink of this fruit of the vine from now on until that day when I drink it anew with you in my Father's kingdom" (Matt. 26:29). In Luke's version, near the end of the Supper he adds, "And I bestow on you a kingdom, just as my Father bestowed one on me, that you may eat and drink at My table in My kingdom . . ." (Luke 22:29-30).

The Eucharistic content of the Last Supper is of course intimately related to the feast of the kingdom. The catholic tradition has always understood the Eucharist to be a foretaste of the kingdom banquet. As such, it manifests that heavenly and future feast within the limits of this present world. By its very nature, then, it presents us with a summons to see beyond itself to the ultimate feast. What is the nature of the supreme feast that is God's kingdom? How might we imagine such a feast? To do so, we must begin with a sense of what an earthly feast is like. Only this can give us an image of that final and unending feast. David Ford has given a richly evocative account of earthly feasting that hints of the absolute feast: "To envisage the ultimate feast is to imagine an endless flow of communication between those who love and enjoy each other. It embraces body language, facial expressions, the ways we eat, drink, toast, dance, and sing; and accompanying every course, encounter and artistic performance are conversations taken up into celebration" (Self, 271).

We will not take the lengthy detour necessary to thoroughly consider this striking description. Certainly, we can observe that its elements and conditions are that of the present world. We may also recognize it as a vision of friendship in a most intensely celebratory realization. In the mystery of such feasting, the whole human being is engaged and expressed in the joyous embrace of supreme interrelatedness and encounter. Traditions of art, music, cuisine, and beverage-making all become media that vivify, embody, support and express the relationship between friends (see Self, 267). Of course, we cannot imagine what exact shape the ultimate feast of God's kingdom will take. But we can imagine that the most complete festal celebration of friendship in this world is but the partial anticipation of what lies ahead and beyond. It is to this that Jesus' words point us.

Friendship in the Kingdom

Paul Wadell has sketched out the relationship between friendship and the kingdom of God with particular emphasis on St. Augustine and the medieval spiritual writer Aelred of Rievaulx. Discussing the classic issue of the relationship between *philia* and *agape*, he comments, "In this way, as Christians grow in agape they do not leave their friendships behind, for the Kingdom is ultimately what their friendships become. The center of their friendships was always Christ, [and] that is why the Kingdom represents not a different love, but an extension of the community formed by that love. This is why we can say the perfect bonding of all men and women in Christ signifies not a love other than friendship, but the unity for which Christian friendship always strove." Quoting Marie A. McNamara on Augustine, he then reaches the ultimate Christological conclusion: "Augustine's ideal of perfect unity is perfect friendship among men who are joined through love inseparably to Christ, so that all together form 'the one Christ loving Himself'" (103).

Wadell points out that Aelred's *Spiritual Friendship* "culminates in this majestic vision of Kingdom unity, where 'with salvation secured, we shall rejoice in the eternal possession of Supreme Goodness; and this friendship, to which here we admit but few, will be outpoured upon all and by all outpoured upon God, and God shall be all in all.'" He goes on to comment: "God's Kingdom is a kingdom of friendship, a Kingdom in which all have perfect unity with one another because all have perfect unity with God. It is not the end of spiritual friendship, it is its perfection; indeed this Kingdom of friendship, humanity of one heart and mind with God, is the unity of all in Christ for which the friends always strove" (110).

Friendship, then, is not a phenomenon that pertains merely to this world. It is not a lesser form of love that grows dim in the light of a greater dawning agape. It is not the indulgence of a preferential exclusivity that must give way to a love more universal. Rather, the love that characterizes true friendship is precisely the kind of love that will be the bond of unity in the everlasting kingdom. The full intensity of love, commitment, devotion, and inner unity that typify the best of friends is an initiation into the communion that all will experience in Christ in the everlasting kingdom. Therefore, to pursue friendships in the beauty of holiness is to drink deeply of the mystery of God's kingdom.

We have noted that there are those who think that *philia* is a love unworthy of the kingdom's perfection. But I maintain with Wadell, Florensky, and others that *philia* is precisely the most eminent precursor of the mutual love between the head and members of Christ's glorified body. Agape, to be sure, is in some ways the most distinctly "Christian" form of love in this fallen world, where love must embrace enemies and the well-being of others must often be purchased at a high price. As such, it imitates the salvific love of Christ for our fallen race. But in the kingdom, the unfortunate conditions which make love a form of sacrifice and self-denial will no longer prevail.

The agape that is salvation in this world will be transformed into the ultimate *philia* of the many within the hypostasis of the one Christ.

Friendship: Sacramental, Mystical, Iconic

A vision of friendship that sees it as a revelation of the ultimate nature of Being and a foretaste of the glories of God's kingdom is a sacramental view of the relationship. Within the framework of Orthodox Christian theology, this affirms it is mystical and iconic. To see friendship in this way is to view it within a greater perspective that sees the phenomena of this world as indicators of and potential bearers of the divine. Philip Sherrard described this viewpoint as the "attempt to express the omnipresence of reality, the penetration of the visible by the invisible, the sensible world by the intelligible" (119).

A distinctly sacramental view of friendship considers it an example of the human bearing the divine. This is not only to say that friendships are a means of grace; it is to hold that friendships offer extraordinary possibilities for growth in the life of Christ and communion with God. Friendship stakes its theological claim on the ground that communion with God is always communion with all others who are in communion with him. Within the constraints of this life, it is not possible that such communion be fully realized with *all* others; however, it may be attained to a high degree of fullness with *certain* others. These are our friends, our fellow-companions on the journey to the kingdom. Through them, in them, and with them, our communion with God strives toward its completion.

The ancient rite of "*adelphopoesis,*" the "making of brothers," witnesses to the sacramental nature of friendship. In spite of the attempt of the late John Boswell to twist this liturgy into an example of "homosexual marriage," it clearly was a rite for the blessing of a friendship.[1] At the heart of this liturgical action lay the conviction that a sacramental rite could recognize two friends as spiritual brothers, or perhaps more to the point, *transform them into* spiritual brothers. This ceremony clearly demonstrates that the Church recognized and sanctified *philia* as a mode of expressing God's kingdom in this world. The fall of this service into desuetude is a poignant reminder of the modern loss of *philia* as a true and godly form of love.

To affirm that friendship has a mystical aspect is to see the deep communion between their souls as an experience of spirit beyond the realm of the empirical and the rational. This means that a historical relationship between persons expressed in the sensible realm through words and actions bears within it an achievement of human self-transcendence. The "experience" of friendship is actually the *experiences* of two distinct persons who nonetheless know that their experience is one. To accept its mystical dimensions is to expressly recognize the transcendental nature of the relationship, and to see that in itself as a manifestation of an even deeper spiritual unity of humanity in the person of the God-man. Ultimately, then, the experience of love between friends becomes the carrier of the experience of the love of Christ. Friendship, as a phenomenon of this world, is not limited by the constraints of the sensible, but is the bearer of the most foundational element of reality. It manifests the Supreme Truth of Being as Communion.

To call friendship "iconic" is to view it in this way, as transparent to the eternal and the divine. It is to see it as a form of love that continually beckons beyond itself. Were friendship to promise to be its own end and fulfillment, it would ultimately be idolatrous. Yet no matter how intense, how powerful, or how captivating, our affectionate attachment toward our friends is, when a friendship calls us to the love of God, it is an icon, not an idol. It enables us to contemplate the invisible and divine through the medium of its humanness and natural sensibility.

The Beauty of Friendship

Because of its inherent sacramental dimensions, friendship beckons us to the very threshold of God's kingdom. The beauty of a genuine soul friendship bespeaks the Ultimate Beauty of the God who is communion. Fr. Thomas Dubay laments that "it is one of the notable sadnesses of our time that so many are incapable of fascination with the deeper levels of human beauty, especially those rooted in the spirit, levels that far transcend physical attractiveness" (64-5). The fellowship between friends, however, is a pathway by which the deeper beauties of the spirit are discovered, revealed, contemplated, and cherished. Discussing the philosophical concept of the "form" as the locus of beauty in art, Dubay quotes Hans Urs von Balthasar: "In order to experience its *form*, a person must become interior to the work, must enter into its spell and radiant space, must attain to the state in which alone the work becomes manifest in its being-in-itself. This holds not only for works of art or the beauties of nature; to an even greater extent it holds for the encounter with a human Thou" (66). This has been exactly our testimony to friendship: it indeed is an entry to the interior reality of another, the radiant space in which that other is known as he truly is. This revelation of the hypostatic reality of the other in the communion of love thus occasions the true contemplation of the beautiful: the human person as image and likeness of God.

Dubay emphasizes that the prerequisite of such seeing is holiness born of love: "Authentic love . . . appreciates in a singular manner the elegance of the beloved" (78). Because of their burning love, he sees the saints as the primary examples of those who are able to become "permeable to and receptive of the deep meanings of things" (79), and thus capable of profound appreciation of the inner beauty of another. He takes up von Balthasar again, affirming that "People who love genuinely can come 'to see their beloved in a wholly different way from others because the beloved's profound interior self is manifested to them in all its utterances and appears as that which is really precious and worthy of love. Every gift, every word, speaks of this, and every reply they give contains their whole self. Exterior exchanges are only bridges by which the souls pass over into one another'"(79).

This is a particularly striking affirmation of the traditional testimony concerning friendship. The contribution of Dubay and von Balthasar is to see this process precisely as an experience of beauty, and an intimation of the Supreme Beauty. As such, then, it buttresses our conviction that friendship is indeed sacramental and offers us a foretaste of heaven. Fired by love and grounded in holiness, genuine Christian friendship passes over from the human to the divine, from this world to the next. It thus bears the character of an eschatological sign; it prefigures the nature of the kingdom of God.

The nature of true friendship is deeply embedded in the fundamental mysteries of the Christian faith. In particular, the Orthodox tradition provides a substantial account of it. Orthodoxy sees the phenomenon of friendship as being rooted in the fact that our humanity has been created "in the image and likeness of God." Thus we are not surprised to see how friendship embodies and witnesses to divine realities. This essential view of friendship then leads to an appreciation of its role in the process of one's salvation. Friendship is seen as having a vital role in the Christian life.

I hope to have portrayed something of the dignity, splendor, and mystery of friendship, and assisted in its restoration to a place of honor in a society that has forgotten ancient pathways of virtuous living. It would be foolhardy to think that friendship will ever generate enough popular fascination to compete with romance and sex; yet for those who understand, the example of Jonathan and David will always speak volumes: "The Lord be between you and me forever." It is this Lord, the undivided Triadic God, who has called us to feast forever in the blessed kingdom of Christ with all others whom we will simply know as "friends."

10 Notes

1. See the discussion of this rite in Florensky, (327-330). He compares the rite of *adelphopoesis* to the marriage ceremony as examples of the Church sanctifying the particular within the context of the communal, and ultimately draws this conclusion: "It is this way in Church life too: the general principle, love, lives not only agapically but also philically, and creates a form for itself – not only the communal liturgy but the *adelphopoesis* of friends" (330). Boswell's work unfortunately was tainted by his political and moral interests (*Same-Sex Unions in Premodern Europe*, New York, 1994).

Epilog

This study has attempted to describe the principles inherent in the nature and conduct of friendship. However, an exclusive concentration on theoretical and moral concerns can never capture the reality of friendship, which is always lived out in real situations by real persons. So as this work began with reflection on a personal moment, it seems fitting to close with a personal anecdote.

As this book was being prepared for publication, a bishop from overseas visited our parish. After he had completed the retreats and seminars, I accompanied him to the airport with our local bishop and a monk. Since September 11, in our local airport it is no longer possible to follow a passenger to the gate. One can only go as far as the foot of the line to the security check. Thus our visiting bishop had to go on alone in the line as we stood at the entrance.

As he moved up in the line, he did a curious thing. On two occasions, he turned fully around with his back to the gate and simply looked at us. He didn't gesture or attempt to communicate. He just looked at us. At that moment, I realized what we all knew: there was a good chance that he would never see us again.

I also realized that in the short time we had spent with him, we had begun to make a friend. Then we were there in the airport, and we had but those final moments to experience a relationship that we had come to cherish.

Oddly enough, only then did I really understand why I had written this book in the first place. I don't know if I really can state it, but it boils down to something like this: That within us that seeks out and sustains friendship is the very essence of being human. The impulse toward communion, the desire for pure love in sheer freedom, and the yearning for eternity — all these are embodied in the discovery of absolute value in another person.

Appendix

Plato, Passion, Personhood and Philia

There is considerable discussion as to the extent to which ancient, medieval and Renaissance expressions of "friendship love" were in fact lightly clothed versions of homoerotic passion. Writing from an acknowledged "gay" perspective, Rictor Norton demonstrates that this is a potent factor not to be summarily discounted (See *The Homosexual Pastoral Tradition* ch. 7: "Faithful Friend and Doting Lover, at http://www.infopt.demon.co.uk/pastor07.htm). There is little doubt concerning the ancient Greeks. Plato's writings are unambiguous in this regard, although Plato definitely rejects homosexual acts as contrary to nature. Nonetheless, in his works, the devotion of *philia* and resulting universal contemplations seem to occur exclusively in the company of handsome young boys, not with aged and grizzled philosophers. Norton, however, makes the typical assumption that whenever there is intense affection and devotion, it must in fact be sexual desire. This is his reading of Montaigne, for instance. While he certainly makes the case that a number of the historical examples in the "friendship tradition" do seem to be expressions of homoerotic passion, he paints with too broad a brush. In our current erotically obsessed cultural situation, it is all too easy to assume that wherever there is intense affection, devotion, and interest in another, it must be a matter of sexual desire. In short, we tend to confuse *philia* with *eros*. Although the boundary between them is indeed thin at times, they are distinct, and it is certainly possible to love another person intensely *as a friend*. In fact, I would argue that our modern preoccupation with sex is partly due to the fact that our culture has forgotten the nature of *philia* and does not make allowance for its expression. This is especially true of northern Europe and North America, where "manliness" is associated with emotional disengagement and the avoidance of touch.

Varied interpretations and estimations of the impact of Plato's views are plentiful even today. Generally, the critique of Plato is that he depersonalizes the object of his affection into a mere image of the beauty of heavenly forms. George Vlastos thus writes, "This seems to me the cardinal flaw in Plato's theory. It does not provide for the love of whole persons, but only for love of that abstract version of persons which consists of the complex of their best qualities . . . When loved as congeries of valuable qualities, persons cannot compete with abstractions of universal significance . . . Plato seems barely conscious of the fact that this "holy image" is himself a valuing subject, a center of private experience and individual preference, whose predilections and choice of ends are no reflex of the lover's" (in Soble, pp.110-111). L.A. Kosman, however, points out that Plato recognized that it is precisely the abstract Idea *incarnate* in the object of love that is the source of contemplation. In other words, the beloved is not devalued as a human person; rather, it is precisely the specific beauty of his humanity as such that is the springboard to *katharsis* and transcendental vision. In this view, Platonic contemplation does not seek to forget the particular once it rises to contemplation of the universal and transcendent. Its goal is to see the particular in the context of the universal and transcendent. This view, with which I am inclined to agree, does not view Plato as involved in an unwarranted abstraction, but rather in contemplation. Meilander seems to read Plato in this way. However, Badhwar and Vlastos appear to be correct in failing to find any genuine appreciation in Plato for the actual characteristics that make the object of *philia* truly *a person.*

Apart from discussing Plato, philosophers have continued to discuss different views of the origin and object of the love of another person. On one hand, there is the problem when one loves another because of his qualities, if it is the qualities that are the primary focus of his love. If this is the case, then the other's *person* is incidental. It is the qualities that are important, and one friend that bears them could conceivably be supplanted by another that bears them to a greater degree. Another view is that one loves his friend and so sees his good qualities in bold relief. He is fond of *them* precisely because he loves *him*. It this view the love is prior. But then the question becomes, "If it is not his qualities, what causes him to love his friend in the first place?"

Undoubtedly, both of these views are philosophical abstractions that bear little relation to the way we actually perceive and value those whom we love. We have no experience of one's good qualities apart from the person in which they inhere, and we have no experience of love for a person apart from knowing certain of his qualities. As Neera Badhwar comments, "No description of an individual's characteristics which abstracts from their style of expression in his particular existence can capture the *person*" (in Soble, 181, italics hers). She stresses the uniqueness of any given person's qualities by noting that each person has his own style of expressing them.

Badhwar's view of "end friendship" (friendship as an end in itself) thus is based on solidly personalist principles. She writes "I have argued that to love a friend as an end is to love her for her intrinsic worth, for the worth that is hers by virtue of her personal nature . . . the love is necessarily based on the qualities that do define the person . . . I have argued that these qualities can neither be, nor be understood, apart from a person's historical and numerical identity" (in Soble, ed., 181-2). In short, she stresses that each person is necessarily unique and irreplaceable, and that friendship is directed to distinct persons who are best described by their defining, rather than incidental, *personal* characteristics. Soble's critique points out how notoriously difficult it is to establish criteria to differentiate "defining" qualities versus incidental ones (see 82). Although this is not the place to elaborate such a justification, I believe such criteria would especially involve the recognition of a person's *habits*, whether spiritual, moral, aesthetic, rhetorical, behavioral, or relational. Also of importance would be his fundamental commitments, his bodily characteristics, and sensibilities. In the end, *philia* is a personal affect directed to other persons.

Bibliography

Berry, Carmen Renee and Traeder, Tamara, *True Blue Friends*, (Andrews McMeel Publishing, Kansas City, MO, 2000).

Berry, Wendell, *Life is a Miracle*, (Counterpoint, Washington, D.C., 2000).

Brown, Peter, *The Body and Society*, (Columbia University Press, New York, 1988).

Burrell, David, *Friendship and Ways to Truth*, (Notre Dame Press, Notre Dame, IN, 2000).

Capsanis, George, *The Eros of Repentance*, (Praxis Institute Press, Newbury, MA, n.d.).

Dubay, Thomas, *The Evidential Power of Beauty*, (Ignatius Press, San Francisco, 1999).

Florensky, Pavel *The Pillar and Ground of Truth*, (Princeton University Press, Princeton, NJ, 1997).

Ford, David, *Self and Salvation*, (Cambridge University Press, New York, 1999).

Ford, David, *The Shape of Living*, (Baker Book House, Grand Rapids, MI, 1997).

Jonopoulos, Collette D., *One Thing Needful*, (Light & Life Publishing, Minneapolis, 1996).

Jung, Carl, *Psychological Types*, (Princeton University Press, 1990).

Keirsey, David and Bates, Marilyn, *Please Understand Me* (Prometheus Nemesis Book Co., Del Mar, CA, 1984).

Krakauer, Jon, *Into the Wild*, (Anchor Books Doubleday, New York, 1996).

Laing, R.D., *Self and Others*, (Penguin Books, New York, 1990).

Lewis, C.S., *The Four Loves*, (Harvest/HBJ Books, New York, 1960).

Lynch, William, S.J., *Images of Hope*, (Notre Dame Press, 1987).

MacMurray, John, *Persons in Relation*, (Humanity Books, Amherst, NY, 1999).

Meilaender, Gilbert, *Friendship: A Study in Theological Ethics*, (Notre Dame Press, 1985).

Mills, David, "Close Your Mind: Critical Christians in an Uncritical Age," in *Touchstone*, vol. 13, no. 8, October 2000.

Pakaluk, Michael, ed., *Other Selves*, (Hackett Publishing Co., Indianapolis, IN, 1991).

Picard, Max, *The Flight from God*, (Gateway Editions, Washington, D.C. 1989).

Rolheiser, Ronald, *The Shattered Lantern*, (Crossroad Publishing, New York 1997).

Schnarch, David, *Passionate Marriage* (Owl Books, New York 1997).

Sherrard, Philip, *Christianity: Lineaments of a Sacred Tradition*, (Holy Cross Orthodox Press, Brookline, MA, 1998).

Soble, Alan, *Eros, Agape, and Philia*, (Paragon House, New York, 1989).

Sophrony, Archimandite, *The Monk of Mount Athos*, (SVS Press, Crestwood, NY, 1973).

Spitzer, Robert J. *Healing the Culture*, (Ignatius Press, San Francisco, 2000).

Sullivan, Andrew, *Love Undetectable*, (Alfred A. Knopf, New York, 1998).

Theophan the Recluse, *Unseen Warfare*, (SVS Press, 1978).

Wadell, Paul, *Friendship and the Moral Life*, (Notre Dame Press, 1989).

White, Carolinne, *Christian Friendship in the Fourth Century*, Cambridge University Press, 1992).

Zizioulas, John, *Being as Communion*, (SVS Press, 1985).